This book is dedicated to
William Sweet, Fernando Pereira, Bartolomeu
Morais da Silva, Mike Hill, Tom Worby, Jill Phipps,
Karel Van Noppen, David Chain, Vicki Moore, Beth
O'Brien, Robert Bryan, Barry Horne, and Adrian
Priscu who have died in defense of innocent life.
You will not be forgotten.
Dedicated also to the brave men and women of the
Liberation underground who risk life and freedom in
defense of innocent life. You are branded as terrorists
by corrupt governments now, but eventually you will
be looked back upon as the heroes who you truly are.
Keep fighting!

Author ~ anonymous ~

The Guide -
a handbook on direct action and activist security

Table of Contents

Getting Started

If you want to take direct action, there are a lot of things to decide upon and a lot of things to keep in mind. The first thing you should ask yourself is whether you want to take legal, aboveground direct action (such as protests) or illegal, underground direct action (such as liberations and economic sabotage). You should focus primarily, if not solely, on aboveground activism or underground direct action, not both. If you become heavily involved in aboveground activism, you will draw government attention and make it much harder for yourself to get away with underground direct action.

If you are currently involved in aboveground activism and want to switch to underground direct action, do not suddenly stop participating in aboveground activism. Slowly back away from it to reduce suspicion and lay low for a while before beginning to take underground direct action.

If you want to become involved in aboveground activism, you can join an existing group or start your own. If you want to get involved in underground direct action, you will probably need to start your own cell. If you know of an existing cell's existence, it has very weak security and will most likely be discovered and infiltrated by government agents. By starting your own cell, you can ensure that it stays secret and that everyone involved is someone who you absolutely trust.

Underground cells typically consist of two to five people but some complex actions such as laboratory raids require more people and some simple actions such as economic sabotage can be carried out by lone wolf activists. Before getting started, you should read this entire guide and, if you feel it is necessary, do additional research. Many sections of this guide are applicable primarily to activists who take underground direct action, but some sections can also be useful to activists who are involved in aboveground activism.

Finding People to Work With

Most activists work in cells, but some prefer to act as lone wolves.

4

If you choose to work with others, finding people who you can trust is extremely important. It only takes one weak link to get everyone in your cell in prison.

-Lone wolf activists have very significant advantages: They completely eliminate the risk of infiltrators and traitors and they do not need to rely on or trust anyone but themselves. However, they also have the disadvantage of not being able to carry out complex actions such as liberations. Some activists may choose to work alone when carrying out economic sabotage but work with a cell when liberating animals.

-Do not trust anyone completely. Everyone has a breaking point, especially when faced with a long prison sentence. Operate on a need-to-know basis.

-When recruiting a cellmate (a person who will be part of your direct action cell), approach the subject of direct action slowly. Casually find out if the person supports direct action before even hinting at your own intentions to take direct action.

-Try to do all of the talking outside without other people or electronic devices such as cell phones nearby. Even at this early stage, you should only choose people who you have known for a long time and have a lot of trust in. It only takes one small mistake to send you to prison for years.

-Before asking a person to take direct action with you, imagine what he/she would do if interrogated or arrested. Would he/she break under pressure? Would he/she turn in you or your cellmates for a reduced sentence, cash reward, or simply because of police harassment? Also consider whether he/she is in good enough physical shape to take direct action and whether he/she will take security seriously enough.

-Only trust people who you have personally known for a long time. Do not trust someone just because a friend claims that the person is trustworthy.

-Do not rely on unreliable people.

-Do not trust someone just because they are willing to do something.

-Only trust Vegans who are very committed to Liberation. Someone who is not willing to do the simple act of giving up things like food and clothing to save innocent lives is obviouly not dedicated enough to the movement and will likely betray you, your cellmates, and the movement.

-Avoid working with people who like to brag, talk, or gossip too much and who make decisions based only on emotion. They will have a hard time keeping quiet.

-Avoid working with alcoholics and drug users. They are too likely to, intentionally or unintentionally, give out information. Even if they are normally very trustworthy, they might say too much when they are drunk.

-Avoid working with people who are involved in other illegal activities. If they are caught for doing something else illegal, they can, will, and have snitched on cellmates to reduce their own sentence.

-There are government agents who have infiltrated the movement and who exist within the movement for the sole purpose of sabotaging activists. These people exist within groups like SHAC and PETA and also outside of groups. They will attempt to infiltrate underground cells. They will attempt to befriend you, encourage you to take direct action (with or without them), and report you. They will pretend to be activists, will pretend to be Vegan and eat Vegan food, will offer to pay for various expenses, and even offer you housing. You can rarely, if ever, be completely sure whether or not a person can be trusted. To minimize your risk of getting tricked by one of these people, use your best judgment and only work with trustworthy friends who you have known for a long time, preferably since before you got involved in the Liberation movement. For more information on infiltrators, read this (http://negotiationisover.com/?p=2190).

-Before talking to anyone about becoming involved in direct action, ensure that the person is not wearing a wire or any type of eavesdropping bug. Wires are usually worn in the small of the back. Instruct the person who you are talking to to lift his/her shirt above his/her head and slowly turn around. Pat down the person's legs. Instruct the person to remove his/her shoes and check them for sound recording devices. Check the person's pockets for sound recording devices.

-Some bugs can be hidden in cigarette packs and other small containers. If the person you are talking to has a small container, open it and ensure that there is not a bug inside of it.

-Do not talk to someone if he/she has a purse, bag, or backpack nearby. This could contain a sound recording device or, even if the person is on your side, an electronic device that the government is tapping.

-If you have a radio frequency detector, use it in case the person has a well-concealed bug.

-You may also want to go through the person's wallet to check for government or police ID cards and ensure that the person is who he/she claims to be. This is not completely accurate because government agents will use fake ID cards and business cards.

-Do not assume that a person is not an infiltrator just because he/she is not wearing a wire. Infiltrators might first try to get information and then bring the topic up again when wearing a wire.

-If possible, try to not let your cellmates know each others' identities, their names, what they look like, where they live, where they work or go to school, or any other information. This will prevent them from betraying you or each other.

-Talk to your cellmates about what would be the hardest for each of you if you are imprisoned so that you can mentally prepare yourself for a worst-case scenario. Be cautious of people who say that they can easily handle a prison sentence because they are usually all talk and they are the people who are most likely to break under pressure.

-After you have formed your cell, you should go through a sort of ritual where every cell member makes a promise or oath to not reveal any information to anyone (other activists, friends, boyfriend or girlfriend, family, cops, agents, or anyone else) and that no information will ever leave the cell. This might help some cell members make it through an interrogation, arrest, trial, or grand jury without giving away any information. Keep in mind that cops might say that they will give you a lighter sentence if you turn in your friends, but they are very likely lying, and how would you feel if your friend goes to prison because of you? Also keep in mind that if your friends stay out, they can continue to take direct action and save more lives. Even if you do not feel you need this ritual, others in your cell might. They may be embarrassed to admit to it so you should do this even if your cellmates say that they do not need it. Repeat this process every time you recruit a new cellmate.

-Make sure everyone in your cell reads this guide, knows how to stay secure, understands the importance of security culture, is familiar with laws and interrogation techniques, and knows what to do if approached by cops or agents or arrested.

Security Culture

Make security your number one priority. Not adhering to a strict security culture means spending years in prison not helping animals.

-DO ALL PLANNING IN REAL LIFE. DO NOT TALK ABOUT DIRECT ACTION IN OR NEAR THE HOME OR VEHICLE OF YOURSELF OR ANOTHER ACTIVIST. DO NOT HAVE ANY CELL PHONES OR OTHER ELECTRONIC DEVICES NEAR YOU. MAKE SURE THAT NO ONE ELSE HAS A CELL PHONE OR OTHER ELECTRONIC DEVICE. BE OUTSIDE IN THE COUNTRY FAR FROM ANYTHING HUMAN-MADE.

-Do not assume that the government is not watching you. If you are an activist, or even just a Vegan, the government is likely already monitoring you. The FBI even goes so far as to infiltrate Vegan potlucks and their terrorist watchlist has approximately 400,000 people on it!

-If you have to discuss direct action in a public location, stay outside and keep walking so that you are more difficult to monitor. Do not discuss direct action if you have any electronic devices with you. If you have to walk past the home or vehicle of yourself or another activist, do not discuss direct action until you are far away from it.

-Never discuss direct action in a building or vehicle under any circumstances. The government has ways of eavesdropping on activists' conversations in houses and vehicles. Whispering and loud background music are not sufficient. Do not rely on radio frequency detectors or radio frequency blockers because they cannot always pick up high-frequency bugs, microphones, or lasers.

-Never discuss direct action via email, instant message, phone, or any other electronic means. The government hacks activists' conversations and activists have been caught this way. The government can trace emails, instant messages, forum posts, and other online activities to the computer and internet service pro-

10

vider even if fake accounts and email addresses are used. Encryption and proxy servers are not always sufficient defenses.

-Do not discuss direct action via mail. The government opens mail. They are especially likely to open your mail if they know that you are a Vegan and/or activist.

-Using code words and/or encryption is not good enough. Some activists were convicted in part because of a text message on one of their phones that said 'Could be a while, the bees are buzzing' implying that there were cops near the place of action. The government will decode your slang and code words will be sure to attract unwanted attention. The government will also decrypt encrypted information transfers and even PGP is not good enough because of the risk of keyloggers and screenloggers.

-The government can track the location and speed of cell phones and other electronic devices, even if their batteries are removed. They can also listen to phone conversations and listen to conversations going on near phones (cell phones and landlines), laptops, and other electronic devices, even if the devices are off, and even whispers. It is unknown whether they have the ability to tap phones with the battery removed. They do not need physical access to your device to do this. It can all be done remotely. For these reasons, phones, laptops, music players, and other electronic devices should never be taken when planning or carrying out direct action.

-When taking direct action, do not use a vehicle with a built-in GPS device or tracking/communications device such as OnStar and do not bring a portable GPS device.

-If you use a vehicle, consider using a radio frequency detector (to detect tracking devices installed by the government) and GPS blocker (to disable tracking devices). Be careful, many detectors do not pick up high-end tracking devices. Some tracking devices only emit a signal every twenty minutes, so a detector should be used for at least twenty minutes to ensure it does not miss picking up a signal. Even good detectors may not be able to detect all tracking devices and should not be relied on, only used as added precautions. Take the same precautions that you would take if not using these devices.

-In addition to using a radio frequency detector and GPS blocker, manually check for tracking devices. Tracking devices have been found on activists' vehicles in the form of tangled wires and electronics attached to the rear bumpers of their vehicles. Tracking devices do not always have the same appearance, so do not overlook something just because it does not fit this description. Check under seats and cushions, under floor mats, on the dashboard, under the steering column, under the gas and brake pedals, under the console, in the glove compartment, in ashtrays, in pouches on seat backs, in compartments in doors, and anywhere else that something could be hidden. Tracking devices are small, sometimes as small as matchbooks. Do not underestimate where they could be hidden. If you find an unfamiliar object, get rid of it right away.

-Even when combined, a radio frequency detector, a GPS blocker, and manually checking for tracking devices will not necessarily reveal or disable all tracking devices. Use these techniques as precautions but always assume that your vehicle is being tracked.

-Operate on a need-to-know basis. Nobody talks and everybody walks. This applies to specific actions and to your general involvement in illegal activities. If someone does not know something, they cannot reveal it (intentionally or unintentionally). Do not tell someone just because they are your best friend, your boyfriend or girlfriend, your parent, or an activist. It is not worth the risk. Everyone has a breaking point. Someone who was not involved in an action is much more likely to break under pressure after being harassed and intimidated because they are not facing prison time. Even if they are trustworthy, they can be tricked by cops and agents (who are experts at social engineering) into giving out incriminating information.

12

-The only people who should know about an action are those who are directly involved. This includes the people who will be taking action and, in some cases, a person with an emergency phone, a person with a safe house or sanctuary, and a veterinarian. Do not even tell cellmates who are not involved in a particular action. People who are involved but will not be directly participating in the action, such as veterinarians and people with safe houses, should only know as much as is necessary.

-Develop the ability to remain silent. This means the ability to refrain from bragging to friends and family even if you trust them and even if they ask about an action or suspect you. This also means the ability to remain silent under intense pressure, including threats, from cops and agents. Most threats from cops and agents are empty threats. Avoid working with people who are unable to remain silent.

-It is NEVER okay to talk about your involvement or someone else's involvement in illegal activities or underground groups, your plans or someone else's plans to become involved in illegal activities, your desire or someone else's desire to become involved in illegal activities, or someone else's advocacy for illegal activities. It is also never okay to ask someone else if they are involved in illegal activities. The only exceptions are when you are planning an action with your cell in a secure location, when submitting an anonymous communique, or if you have been caught and have served your entire sentence.

-Do not talk about other activists if you are unsure if what you want to say about them is public knowledge, even if it is something that you think cannot get them in trouble. This applies whether it is rumor/speculation or personal knowledge.

-Do not give out names to ANYONE (government or not) under ANY circumstances. Even if you are only being asked about people involved in aboveground activism or even something as seemingly harmless as who your friends are, SAY NOTHING. Remain silent and TAKE NO RISKS.

-Do not talk about an action just because you get caught. Do not say anything acknowledging your involvement such as 'How did they catch us?' or even something as seemingly harmless as 'What happened?' unless you are in a secure location. Do not say anything that could help the government identify who you took action with. There might not be solid proof that you are responsible so you could still get off the hook if you do not talk. This applies whether or not you have been convicted and whether or not you have already served part of your sentence. Admitting to an action can also help the government track down other members of your cell.

-If you have served your entire sentence and been released, it is okay to discuss your actions, but do not mention who you took action with or give law enforcement any clues as to who you took action with.

-Do not talk about an action to anyone, even others who were involved, after it has been carried out. This is especially important for high-risk actions such as laboratory raids, arsons, firebombings, bombings, and anything involving violence. A large percentage of convicted ALF and ELF activists were caught because of traitors and infiltrators. If you absolutely have to talk about a past action, take the same precautions that you would take if planning a new action. Some investigations will last for years.

-Snitches and infiltrators are one of the most dangerous threats to underground activists. The government will pay a former activist to wear a wire and try to get information out of old friends or will pay someone to pretend to be an activist and infiltrate the movement. Infiltrators also try to disrupt groups and create infighting with the movement. This is sometimes, ironically, done by advocating witch-hunts for infiltrators and traitors. Other times it is done by accusing activists of other things that they have not done or by creating splits based on race, gender, class, or sexual orientation. If someone brings up an old action, do not say anything that you would not want the government to hear and consider whether that person is possibly a traitor and should be cut off from your cell. If someone acts suspiciously enthusiastic about taking direct action, suggests doing something that would compromise security, or suggests doing something very extreme, consider whether that person is possibly an infiltrator.

-Do not try to expose someone without solid proof of the person being an agent and verify rumors of infiltrators before acting on them. If you need help determining whether or not someone is an infiltrator, get help from as few people as possible to minimize the risk of false rumors. In the case of a potential traitor or infiltrator, check the person for a wire or other sound recording device. For more information on detecting infiltrators, see Finding People To Work With.

-Do not let stress, anxiety, anger, or impatience make you act impulsively. If you do, you will be caught. Always put security first.

-Put personal issues aside. If you have an issue with another member of your cell, maybe it is best for everyone that you leave the cell or at least talk out your problems. There is no room for personal feelings or power issues to get in the way of an action.

-If you are a member of more than one cell, do not reveal the identity of the members of one cell to the members of the other cell. Neither cell should even know that the other exists or that you are involved in another cell. Never mix cells. The only exception is when it is absolutely necessary such as if you need more people than exist in either cell alone. If this happens, attempt to not let one cell's members learn the identities of the members of the other cell. Talk to all of the members of each cell before planning the action to ensure that they are alright with mixing cells.

-If someone in your cell does anything to compromise security or does not take security culture seriously enough, explain to them why they cannot do what they are doing. Do not try to sound like you are better than them. Make sure that you sound helpful and like you have their best interest in mind. Talk to the person in private, out of earshot of your other cellmates. Acting like you are superior or embarrassing them in front of your other cellmates will make them not want to listen and will make them much more likely to continue compromising security.

-If they do not stop compromising security after being talked to about it, you have to stop working with them. They are too much of a risk to you, your cell, themselves, and the entire movement.

-Some examples of security-compromising behaviours are:
  --Lying: An activist might claim to have done something illegal to impress others. The police will not take it as a lie.
  --Gossiping: Some people have a hard time refraining from accidentally giving out information. Avoid them. They are a danger to you, your cell, and the movement.
  --Creating and spreading rumors: If someone does not know who is responsible for an action, they might make an assumption as to who is responsible and tell others. This may or may not regard an action carried out by your cell. This may be due to a person thinking that they can make friends by having secret information. It may also be due to government speculation as to who carried out an action.
  --Bragging: Some people will brag about an action to friends or family to sound good, be accepted, or because they think they can make friends by having secret information.
  --Indirect bragging: Some people will hint at having done an action for the same reasons as directly bragging. This is very dangerous because cops and agents are extremely skilled at gathering information.
  --General lack of concern: Some people do not care enough about security in general and do not take security culture seriously. This is extremely dangerous to everyone in your cell.

-Do not write down anything about your actions, anywhere.This means no diary entries. This means no information saved on your computer. (Files can be recovered from a hard drive even after being permanently deleted.) The only exception is when sending anonymous communiques.

-Many activists choose to write communiques after taking action. The purposes of writing a communique can include documenting an action, explaining the intentions behind an action, rleasing useful information gained during an action, and motivating or encouraging other activists to take direct action.

-Before sending a communique, talk to your cellmates to ensure that none of them is also planning to send one.

-If you send a communique, consider naming the action in honor of activists who are currently imprisoned (specifically those with the longest and most outrageous sentences and who have a large portion of their sentence ahead of them) or who have been starved and/or murdered. This will discourage the government from giving out such long sentences because they will fear more sympathy actions. You can say that you will continue to take action in honor of this person/people as long as they are imprisoned, possibly getting them an early release.

-If you send a communique, you may not want to sign it as the ALF, ELF, or any other existing group. If you are caught, you will be given a longer prison sentence and heavier fines simply for being part of a 'terrorist organization'. You may also want to avoid sending an extremely militant communique and avoid including threats to animal abusers for similar reasons.

-If you choose to sign the communique, remember that the Animal Liberation Front and Earth Liberation Front are strictly nonviolent. If your action involves violence and you want to claim it in the name of a group, you can use a name such as Animal Rights Militia, Earth Liberation Army, Revolutionary Cells, or Justice Department.

-If you send a communique, refrain from using the same writing style and phrases you typically use. For example, if you commonly say 'Go Vegan or die!' do not put that in the communique. You can also use bad grammar, capitalization, and punctuation if you normally use good and vice versa. Do not include any information that could be used to identify the names, ages, genders, races, or anything else related to you or your cellmates. Sending a short, concise communique will make it harder for you to be identified based on writing style.

-Make sure that if you include photos or videos with your communique they do not reveal tattoos, eyes, or any other identifying information.

-Photos and videos may include embedded data revealing what camera they were taken with, the location and time they were taken, and other identifying information. This information will not be obviously visible but can be discovered by the government.

-Remove sound from video footage, or at very least add fake background noises, and make other changes to photos and videos to mislead the government.

-Only send communiques to groups like:
  --Bite Back (DirectAction.info) and
  --NAALPO (AnimalLiberationPressOffice.org).
Their contact information (mailing address, email address, and PGP key) is available on their websites. If you send a communique to the media, the police will try to trace it (through various means such as forensics, handwriting, and computer tracing) and might succeed. Also, media coverage is biased against direct action and depicts activists as criminals and terrorists.

-If you send a communique via internet (which is strongly discouraged), research internet security and anonymity. Do not use an email account that is linked to you. Use a different password, name, address, birthday, and other information than you use on other accounts. Make sure that you have no keyloggers or screenloggers on your computer. Files can be recovered from a hard drive even after being deleted and there is no completely accurate way to detect keyloggers and screenloggers so there is always some risk involved in sending a communique via internet or even typing and printing a communique to mail. If for any reason you have to print something, use notepad to eliminate meta data present in other filetypes such as .doc and .pdf.

-If you send a communique from your home computer, use TrueCrypt (http://www.truecrypt.org/downloads), a secure Linux-based operating system such as Ubuntu (http://www.ubuntu.com/), a MAC address randomizer such as MAC Changer (http://www.alobbs.com/macchanger), a secure browser such as Firefox (http://www.mozilla.com/), Tor (https://www.torproject.org/), and PGP (http://www.pgp.com/) or GPG (http://www.gnupg.org/). Encryption, proxies, and other security measures do not guarantee complete security because there are still risks such as keyloggers and screenloggers.

-If you send a communique from a public internet service, be out of view of security cameras and make sure that no one is watching you. Be careful to not leave fingerprints on the keyboard or mouse. Wear clothing that conceals your identity without looking obvious and/or wear clothing of a style that is completely different from what you normally wear. For example, if you are a punk rock scene kid, wear New Age clothes. Do not log on to any accounts that are linked to you while on this computer. Do not visit any websites that you regularly visit. Do nothing except for type and send the communique.

-If you send a physical communique (this is recommended because the government is good at hacking), security is still very important. The government opens mail addressed to Animal Liberation and Earth Liberation groups (such as Bite Back and NAALPO) and mail addressed to activists so there should be no way to trace the communique to you.

-If you send a physical communique, use very basic stamps, envelopes, and paper or buy stamps, envelopes, and paper specifically for the communique and dispose of the rest. Be careful to not be seen disposing of the rest. Pay with cash and burn the receipt. It is worth it to be a little wasteful if it means staying out of prison and continuing to be an activist. Use a 0.7mm graphite pencil or a basic black or blue ballpoint pen. Pilot pens are recommended because some other companies test on animals and use aimal-derived adhesives in their ink.

-If you send a physical communique, do not use your regular hand-writing. Use capital block letters with no curves. See here (http://www.directaction.info/news_dec19_09.htm) for an example. You can use a stencil, but if you do, the stencil should be purchased specifically for the communique and disposed of afterwards. Do not type and print a communique because there are various ways to trace it to you whether you use a public or private computer.

-Burn drafts of the communique as well as several sheets of paper which were underneath it and will contain imprints.

-When purchasing paper, envelopes, and stamps and when writing and handling a physical communique, be very careful to not contaminate the letter, envelope, stamp, or any enclosed materials such as photos with DNA. Wear latex gloves and cotton gloves (fingerprints can be left through latex gloves and sweat, containing DNA, can soak through cotton gloves). Wear a hat. If you have long hair, tie it back. Do not lick the stamp or envelope. Use self-stick stamps or use an unused wet sponge. Seal the envelope with an unused wet sponge or tape. Use tape cautiously because it is good at attracting hair which contains DNA.

-Do not use a return address or use a fake return address. Make sure there are enough stamps.

-Mail the communique from a public drop-box far from your home and do not be seen on security cameras when you put it in. If it is cold enough to wear gloves without looking suspicious, do. If it is too warm, hold the communique between blank envelopes or put it in a large manila-style folder until you get to the drop-box. Be careful to not look suspicious and do not let the communique touch your fingers as you drop it in. Be careful to not drop the blank envelopes or manila folder into the drop-box.

-Ideally, underground activists should not possess direct action guides or militant literature. If you do own these things, never keep them anywhere that they can be easily seen and, if possible, keep them at the house of a trustworthy friend who supports, but does not partake in, illegal direct action. This friend should not know that you partake in underground direct action. Your house could be raided at any time.

-Underground activists should not be very outspoken in support of direct action, should not wear shirts with the ALF logo or any other direct action words or symbols, should not be heavily involved in aboveground activism (especially that which is related to Animal Liberation or Earth Liberation), and should not in any other way draw attention to themselves. Aboveground activists and outspoken supporters of direct action draw government attention and are almost guaranteed to be heavily monitored.

-If you live with relatives, roommates, or anyone else who is not involved in the Liberation underground, do not let them suspect you of underground direct action. Come up with believable excuses for being out (that kind of lying is okay because it keeps you out of prison and allows you to keep helping animals). If anyone suspects you of being involved in direct action, whether it is family, roommates, friends, police, or anyone else, stop taking direct action and lay low for a while, even if you trust the person who suspects you. Only start taking direct action again when the suspicion has subsided.

-If your life begins to revolve around activism, you may want to consider being homeless or living with a friend. Without an address, phone, or house, you are harder to monitor and harder to find. Do not rely on this to remain anonymous; simply use it as an added precaution.
-Read all of the topics in the ALF Security Forum (http://www.ani-

malrightsdiscussion.com/Forum/forumdisplay.php?f=113) and look through the articles on the ALF site (http://www.animalliberationfront.com/). It is better to spend a few hours reading about your legal rights and security than to spend years in prison (not helping animals!).

-Be extremely cautious. Caution is key. Be extremely secure and make sure that there is no one around when you plan and carry out actions.

-Do not get caught. If there is a high chance of getting caught, do not take the risk. You will do the animals no good if you are sitting in prison.

Choosing a Target

If possible, keep actions to locations that are not near your home. Many activists drive across several states to take direct action. Go as far away as possible. This is especially important for high-risk actions such as laboratory raids, arsons, firebombings, bombings, and anything involving violence. It is also especially important if you are involved in aboveground activism because this will make you a suspect if you live near the place of action even if there is no evidence against you.

-Do not choose targets in any type of pattern or you will be mapped.

-You will be the most effective if you target a weak point within an industry. For example, destroying a fur research facility will have a devastating effect on the fur industry because there are very few left.

-Targeting consumers through aboveground outreach is most effective against the meat, milk, and egg industries because they are very large industries and so many people financially contribute to them. Aboveground activism can also be very effective against fur, leather, and circuses, because many people do not realize how much cruelty is involved and, unlike laboratories, these industries rely solely on consumers.

-Targeting suppliers through protests and underground direct action is most effective against smaller industries. These include fur farms, laboratories, circuses, breeders (including laboratory animal breeders and puppy/kitten mills), leather farms, and fast food restaurants. For example, there are only a few dozen animal circuses left, and a single action could shut down a whole circus forever, meaning that it would only take a few dozen actions to end animal circuses completely.

-Possible targets include:
--Restaurants (especially fast food chains which are symbols of both animal exploitation and capitalism)
--Farms (fur, meat, milk, eggs, leather, wool, honey, and silk)

--Slaughterhouses
--Circuses (make sure that your target is a circus that still uses animals)
--Breeders
--Zoos
--Hunters and hunts
--Hunting lodges and stands
--Trappers
--Fish, whale, and seal killing ships
--Crush film producers
--People who capture wild animals for 'pets' and zoos
--Laboratories
--Government/military laboratories
--Animal transport vehicles (factory farms, circuses, breeders, zoos, and lab animal suppliers)
--Logging companies
--Logging trucks
--Offshore oil drilling companies
--Banks and other capitalist institutions
--Companies affiliated with any of the above (equipment suppliers, feed suppliers, transport/postal services, banks, shareholders, and other business partners)
--The people affiliated with the above, their vehicles, and their homes

-If you do not have a specific target in mind, you will be able to find one at one of these pages:
--The Blueprint (http://www.directaction4.info/Blueprint.pdf)
--The Final Nail (http://www.finalnail.com/)
--Flashpoint Volume I: Animal Research Labs (http://www. scribd. com/full/5688474?access_key=key-ycume39lfodpt5naqfy)
--Flashpoint Volume II: Lab Animal Breeders (http://www.scribd. com/full/5688480?access_key=key-1f52vulaw2yfjgf29gl1)
--Flashpoint Volume III: Slaughterhouses (http://www.scribd.com/ full/5688488?access_key=key-29jdoikl1uy3esuw3tol)
--Flashpoint Volume IV: Fur Farms (http://www.scribd.com/full/ 6193059?access_key=key-11koy9b8t7s80vb46kn2)
--Facility Reports and Information (http://www.all-creatures.org/ saen/res-fr.html)

--US Government Facilities that do Research on Animals (http://www.all-creatures.org/saen/res-usgfac.html)

--Vivisectors(http://www.primatelabs.com/vivisectors.php)

-If you are deciding between several similar targets, choose the one that will involve a lowest risk of getting caught. If you know that one location does not have very much security, go there. If one location is in a town and another is not, target the one that is not. If one is near a police station and the other is not, target the one that is not. If one is in a business area/financial district of a city and the other is in a residential area, target the one that is in a residential area.

-If you are deciding between several fur farms, target one at which the owner's house and the cages are far apart. Liberated animals can make a lot of noise. Also target a farm without a surrounding fence to make it easier for the animals to escape.

-If you are deciding between several laboratories, decide based on the types of experiments being done, knowledge of security weaknesses, and safe homes arranged for certain species of animals.

-Before taking action, ensure that you are targeting the correct location. If you are targeting a home, office, vehicle, or similar target, do not simply rely on a phone call or address book to confirm the address of your target. Do plenty of research.

Choosing an Action
Start with low risk actions such as gluing locks, painting Animal Liberation messages, destroying hunting stands, or even something as simple as deactivating traps that you come across. Start by doing only one thing per action. Work up to doing multiple small things like gluing locks, painting walls, and breaking windows all at once. When you are comfortable with that, move up to mid- risk actions such as raiding fur farms with minimal security. Wait until you are very experienced to raid high security laboratories. You are of no use to animals and Earth if you are in prison.

-You do not have to arson, sabotage, vandalize, and liberate all at the same time. Liberation alone is just fine anddoes not risk as long of a prison sentence.

-Possible actions include:
--Leafleting
--Protesting (office demos and home demos)
--Office/site occupation
--Chalking sidewalks
--Banner drops
--Changing legislation (only effective for no-kill laws, anti-crush laws, and laws regarding activists such as the AETA; animal welfare laws are worthless)
--Rioting
--Hacking industry websites
--Electronic sit-ins (http://www.animalliberationfront.com/ALFron t/Actions-cyberspace/Cyberspace-index.htm)
--Hunt sabbing
--Liberation (from industries and from abusive 'owners')
--Rescuing injured, orphaned, abandoned, stray, and abused animals
--Vandalism (destroy or remove circus/zoo/product advertisements, cover advertisements with Liberation messages or stickers, remove circus/zoo/product coupons, destroy windows, glue locks, paint Liberation messages, paintbomb billboards, pour paint or other damaging substances on fur coats, destroy hunting stands, destroy fur farm breeding cards, destroy or confiscate laboratory data, destroy vehicles, destroy buildings)
--Poison hoaxes (animal products and animal-tested products)
--Bomb hoaxes
--Arson, firebombing, and bombing
--Leaving 'gifts' on animal abusers' doorsteps, under their vehicles, or in their mailboxes
--Razorblades, poison, and letterbombs sent to abusers
--Gathering intelligence (locations, floor plans, security devices, ways to bypass security devices, time (hour and day) andlocation that people (employees, guards, police, and anyone else) are nearby, types of animals kept in laboratories and farms)

--Informing neighbours, friends, and families of animal abusers (painting messages on abusers' garages and houses, chalking nearby sidewalks, protesting, handing out leaflets)

-If you still have a hard time deciding what to do, read this (http://negotiationisover.com/2009/12/27/4688/) for more specific ideas.
-For very detailed information on strategic monkeywrenching, read Ecodefense(http://theanarchistlibrary.org/HTML/Various_Authors __Ecodefense__A_Field_Guide_to_Monkeywrenching.html).

How To Dress And What To Bring
Buy clothing and equipment at separate locations shortly before the action. Supplies should not be purchased near the place of action. Supplies should not be purchased online.

-All gear, including clothing, flashlights, spraypaint cans, tools, and everything else, should be generic, common brands to make it harder to identify.

-Pay with cash and burn the receipts. Remove and burn tags and serial numbers.

-Everything should be purchased specifically for the action and used only for the action.

-Wear gloves when purchasing supplies to avoid getting fingerprints on them if it is cold enough to not look suspicious.

-Wash your supplies as soon as you get home, put them in clean bags, and only handle them with gloves on. Be careful of things like batteries in flashlights that may have fingerprints.

-Wear very basic clothes with no logos and be fully covered. Wear a black hoodie, black sweatpants or blue jeans, a black ski mask, black gloves, black socks, and basic black shoes or boots with black laces and no logos.

-Wear cotton clothes. Nylon is noisy. Cotton is quiet, flexible, and comfortable.

-A ski mask with no nose or mouth holes and eye holes rather than a slit is recommended. It makes you harder to identify and eliminates the risk of an eye slit becoming too wide and revealing your identity. Lack of nose and mouth holes also reduces the risk of leaving behind DNA if you cough or sneeze.

-A hoodie is recommended so that you can wear a ski mask and hood, especially if you have long hair or need a hood to cover a headlamp, but a long-sleeved t-shirt is also acceptable for some low-risk situations. If you have long hair, brush it and tie it back.

-Do not rely on your hood. A ski mask is a necessity. You may be seen on security cameras or your hood may fall down if it is snagged or if you have to run.

-Wear electrician gloves, or latex gloves under plain cotton gloves (preferably with rubber grips and very basic with no patterns or logos). Latex gloves do not prevent fingerprints from being left and can tear easily. Sweat, containing DNA, can soak through cotton gloves. The two should always be combined. Latex gloves with cotton gloves are more flexible than electrician gloves and are harder to identify because they are not as unique, but even with a double layer, there is some risk of sweat soaking though, and they do not offer your hands any protection. If you will be using your hands for a lot, you can use thick work gloves. They are not as bulky as electrician gloves but they provide more protection than thin cotton gloves. If you have to cut through or climb an electric fence or a barbed wire fence, cut or handle electrical wiring, or need waterproof gloves, electrician gloves are necessary. If you are going to be liberating animals, wear gloves that cannot be penetrated by teeth or claws so that you do not leave blood. Wear thick gloves when carrying out major actions such as laboratory raids and arsons to avoid any risk of identification.

-When picking out shoes or boots, some things to consider are leather free, good support, comfortable for running and sprinting, good grip /slip resistant, water proof, and resistant to chemicals and electrical wires. Sketchers makes work shoes with most or all of these traits.

-Make sure that your clothing, especially your mask,fits securely and will not slide down.

-Make sure that your shoes or boots fit very tightly and have very good support in case you have to run from the police.

-Optionally wear thick socks over your shoes to make your footprints less recognizable. The socks should be big enough and thick enough to not rip. Prints will still be somewhat recognizable so shoes should still be burned, especially after high-risk actions.

-Do not wear clothes with tears or stains. They can be used to identify you.

-Do not wear clothes with the ALF logo. They can be used to identify you and they link you to the ALF which can give you a longer sentence if you are caught.

-If you have tattoos, injuries, scars, or anything else that can be used to identify you, make sure that it is covered. Avoid getting tattoos in places like wrists and ankles in case your sleeves or pants slide up. You may also want to avoid getting Liberation related tattoos anywhere because they might be used against you if you are suspected of direct action.

-Optionally wear knee and elbow pads in case you have to crawl a lot, especially in case you are chased by police. For example, you may have to crawl through a hole in a fence as a possible escape route.

-If you wear a headlamp, put it over your ski mask and under your hood so that it cannot be seen as easily by security cameras or witnesses.

-If you are not of the same skin color as most people in your area, do not let your skin be seen. Wear sunglasses, but not the same style you normally wear. They should be purchased specifically for the action and disposed of after the action. Make sure they cannot fall off because they might have hair or sweat that can be traced to you.

-You may want to wear sunglasses regardless of your skin color. The FBI has measured the distance between eyes and pupils to identify people.

-If you have long hair, it should be under your mask and hoodie. You do not want it to be seen on security cameras and you definitely do not want any falling out at the place of the action.

-Wear watches if you plan to split up so you know when to regroup. Synchronize the watches before the action.

-If you wear a backpack, it should be a good quality backpack that will not rip. It should be solid black and not have any logos.

-In some situations, it is a good idea to wear a mask or bandanna and hat at aboveground protests because FBI and police have been known to spy on protests and make logs of protesters. This is especially important if you are also involved in illegal direct action so that you do not draw any unwanted attention. However, it is illegal to wear a mask in public in some states and countries.

-If you want to be anonymous at a protest, wear a plain shirt, plain pants, a bandana and a hat. Alternatively, especially if masks are illegal in your area, you can wear fake scars and a wig (but make sure that they are convincing and that the scars will not peel and that the wig will not slide up or fall off). A hat and bandanna combination is sufficient for a protest but is not sufficient for underground direct action for which a full face ski mask is a necessity.

-Do not bring anything that can be used to identify you or your friends, such as jewelry, a wallet, an address book, or an ID card.

Jewelry can be seen if you wear it and any of these things could be dropped. Leave these things, along with cell phones and other electronic devices, at home. If you are married, you should take off your wedding ring and leave it at home in case you lose a glove. Make sure that your pockets are empty. If you wear a watch, buy one specifically for the action and dispose of it afterwards. This applies to underground direct action and to protests where you want to be anonymous. You may also want to avoid carrying an ID card in your non-activist life in case you are searched or detained and do not want to reveal your identity.

-Some activists record their direct actions with a camera or camcorder. This should only be done if your target is small enough and you have enough activists that using one person to record the action will not reduce the amount of animals liberated or the amount of damage done. If you use a camera or camcorder and can afford it, it should be purchased specifically for the action and disposed of after the action. Cameras and camcorders can be caught on security cameras and photos and video footage contain data which may be able to link them to your camera.

-Do not carry a keychain or anything else that can jingle. After getting dressed, you may want to jump a few times to make sure that you do not make any noise.

-Cover headlamps and flashlights with red screens. This makes them barely visible from a distance.

-Mount a plastic pistol-grip handle on your can of spraypaint. This will ensure that the paint sprays in the direction of the target and not towards you (which would be incriminating).

-If carrying out arson, do not use petrol/gasoline. It is too volatile. Kerosene is less dangerous. Kerosene is available at some petrol/gasoline stations. When purchasing kerosene, use an approved container.

-For detailed instructions on making a simple and cheap incendiary device, refer to pages 16 and 17 of the Animal Liberation Primer (http://animalliberationpressoffice.org/publications%20online/ALprimer3.pdf).

-Do not assume that fingerprints and DNA are not an issue because you are carrying out arson. Something could backfire and prevent your incendiary devices from working. Like all other supplies, incendiary devices should be free of fingerprints and DNA.

-If the route you will be taking is unfamiliar to you (which it should be, because you will be taking remote side roads) bring a detailed road map. The map should be of a large area, such as a whole state, because if it is of a more specific area it is too suspicious. Do NOT put any markings on the map.

-Keep your tools in a plastic bag until you use them and put them back in the bag immediately after using them. Only handle them with gloves on. This will keep them free of fingerprints and DNA so that you can dump them in a dumpster.

-Only bring the gear that you really need. Extra gear weighs you down and is at risk of being left behind and traced to you. Even if it is not unique, it probably contains DNA.

-When possible, use small, compact gear that can be easily carried. In some cases, this may not be an option. It is sometimes necessary to have both small wire cutters and large bolt cutters.

-Use good quality gear. This is especially important for things like walkie talkies, drills, and drill bits.

-Make sure that you bring all of the gear that you will need. Some things to consider include: (make sure that all electronic devices have fresh batteries)
--Black ski mask
--Black hoodie
--Black sweatpants

--Black gloves
--Black socks
--Black shoes or boots
--Sunglasses
--Watches
--Spare clothes and shoes
--Waterproof jacket and pants
--Black backpack
--Knee and elbow pads
--Headlamps or flashlights with red screens
--Compasses
--Binoculars (preferably with night vision)
--Camera or camcorder to record action
--Walkie talkies (be careful--cops may pick up the frequency if they are in the area)
--Pepper spray (in case you are approached by cops or anyone else)
--A reliable vehicle with a full petrol/gasoline tank (optionally rented or borrowed, but keep in mind that many rental vehicles have built-in GPS devices and tracking devices such as OnStar)
--Spare keys
--Spare tires
--Jumper cables
--Vehicle breakdown and recovery information/manual
--Air freshener for vehicle (to mask scent of liberated animals)
--Unmarked detailed road map (if you mark the location it can be used against you)
--Unmarked detailed map of action location
--Driver's license, proof of insurance, and other required documents in case you are pulled over
--Radio scanner/police scanner (to monitor local and state law enforcement frequencies)
--Radio frequency detector (to detect tracking devices and bugs)
--GPS blocker (to disable tracking devices and bugs)
--Cages, sacks, or stackable plastic storage tubs to put lierated animals in until you can get to woods or a field
--First aid kit (for activists or liberated nonhumans)
--Plastic bags for disposal of equipment and to put dirtyclothes in

--Bolt cutters
--Wire cutters
--Pliers
--Lock pick
  --Superglue in pointed tube (with cut up paperclips for added effectiveness in gluing locks)
--Spraypaint can with plastic pistol-grip handle
--Paint bombs
--Paint-filled squirt gun (with plastic bag and rubber band to prevent paint from dripping)
--Glass etching fluid
--Paint brush
--Rocks or bricks
--Slingshot or BB gun with ammo (to break glass)
--Knife or dagger (to slash tires)
--Hammer
--Sledgehammer
--Axe
--Pickaxe
--Saw
--Chainsaw
--Buzzsaw
--Drill with changeable battery and spare battery pack
--Crowbar
--Money to bribe witnesses (including security guards and cops)
--Dog treats to bribe guard dogs
--Hoax bombs
--Butane bombs
--Pipe bombs
--Incendiary devices
--Matches or fresh lighter (not Bic--Bic tests on animals)
--Methocel, oil, or BBs (to slow down people giving chase, especially in narrow areas such as hallways)
--Butyric acid (horrible smell will deter people)

-Decide ahead of time who will bring what supplies. Make sure that everyone knows what they are supposed to bring. You do not want to get to your target and find out that no one brought the bolt cutters.

-Make sure that everyone remembers to bring all of their own gear. If someone forgets gloves or a mask, they will not be able to take action.

-If no one in your cell can afford supplies, you may be able to get money or supplies from someone else. This should be someone who you fully trust and who supports direct action. Do not tell this person about actions before they are carried out. It is best if the person is not told at all, but if the person has to know, give them newspaper clippings or tell them about the actions in a secure location after the actions are carried out. Be careful to not be tricked by an infiltrator who will give you money for supplies in turn for you telling him/her about your actions.

-Keep your suspicious items in non-suspicious locations. Do not hide them because they will probably be found if your house or vehicle is raided. Keep your ski mask with other winter clothes, your bolt cutters and hammer in the garage with other tools (buy other tools to make it less suspicious if necessary), put your superglue in a drawer with scissors and other office supplies, and do similar things for other clothing and equipment. This should only be temporary because clothing and supplies should be purchased shortly before the action and destroyed or disposed of shortly after the action.

-Do not bring a cell phone, laptop, or any other electronic device, and make sure that no one else does. Most cell phones and some laptops have built-in GPS tracking devices. Many of the tracking devices work even with the phone or laptop turned off and the battery removed. Electronic devices can also be tapped even when turned off and possibly even with the battery removed.

Tactics And Strategy

Decide exactly what you want your action to accomplish before working out the finer details. Do not take direct action just for the sake of taking direct action. Make your action as effective as possible. Factor in cost of supplies, risk of getting caught, and how long of a sentence you will get if caught. For example, do not arson if you can do the same amount of damage without fire. Arsons involve more intensive investigations, a higher risk of getting caught, heavier potential fines, and longer potential prison sentences. Do not waste resources and do not take needless risks.

-Make sure the benefits outweigh the costs and risks. If you burn down a hunter's lodge, you risk killing insects, rodents, and companion animals in the lodge, and even setting the surrounding area on fire. If you do something that you are likely to get caught for, you might go to prison and be unable to help as many animals in the future. If you use your time, money, and/or resources poorly, you will end up saving less animals.

-Consider what effect the action will have on the movement. Will it gain public support or lose public support? Does it matter? Will government and industry retaliate or give in?

-Choose your target strategically. If you glue locks at a McDonalds restaurant but there are no follow-up actions against McDonalds restaurants by your cell or others, it will not have nearly as much of an impact as hitting a target that is already subject to an Animal Liberation campaign. Companies will shrug off single actions but they can be shut down by aggressively and relentlessly targeting the same company multiple times using a variety of tactics, including aboveground protests and underground direct action.

-If you are staying overnight away from home, do not stay at a hotel. Stay in a tent at a campsite without many people.

-Carry out your actions at night (preferably between 2:00am and 4:00am) so that there are not many witnesses around who might call the police or identify you.

-If possible, carry out your actions on stormy nights. This makes you harder to be heard and seen and there will be less potential witnesses outside. If a stormy night is not an option, you can take action on an overcast night or a new moon to make you harder to see or, if your action is taking place outside, you can take action on a full moon to eliminate the need of flashlights.

-If you are staying at a hotel (which is discouraged) or taking action near your home, leave the evening before the action. It will look suspicious if you leave late at night the night the action is carried out. This is especially important if you live in an apartment or near buildings with security cameras.

-If you return home immediately after the action rather than waiting until the morning, do not turn on or use your phone or computer when you get home. Turning them on in the middle of the night after an action occurs will raise suspicion.

-Leave time between actions. The police are going to be intensely watching local activists after an action and will notice who is out the night of the next action if it is shortly after the previous one. The police have been known to watch specific activists for months at a time and to follow activists long distances. This is especially important if there are not many activists in your area and you carry out actions near your home.

-Optionally use a fake license plate. This is illegal so use this tactic with extreme caution. If you are pulled over and the cop looks up your license plate number, the computer will display the model of your vehicle. Color is not an issue because vehicles can be painted. If you have a vehicle that looks new and is a current model, you can use a sheet of paper that car dealerships put on vehicles in place of a license plate. Keep in mind that the cop may notice if your odometer has a lot of miles, making it suspicious that you do not yet have a real license plate. If the cop demands to see your proof of insurance that could also give you away.

-Assign a leader in case someone needs to make split second decisions. For example, what if the police see you? Do you fight back or run? Do you stay as a group or scatter? The leader's role should only come into play in emergency situations.

-If your plan involves your group splitting up, assign a leader to each small group. Remember to assign one of these leaders to the entire group for the time that you are all together. The leader of the large group should also be the leader of one of the small groups to avoid confusion as to who is leader at what time.

-If your plan involves your group splitting up, work in groups of two or more so that you can watch each others' backs, to reduce the risk of getting lost, and so that you are with someone if things go wrong and you have to run from cops or if you get lost.

-Do not use more people than necessary, but do not leave out important positions such as lookouts. Extra people means more risk of getting caught, more risk of getting separated during the action, more people at risk, and a higher risk of traitors and infiltrators. Lone wolf actions are ideal when possible because they make it extremely hard for the government to find out who is responsible. They will still find you if you compromise security so do not think that you are invincible just because you are working alone or in a small cell of trustworthy people.

-It is especially important to have a minimum number of people involved in actions with a high risk of getting caught or heavy potential charges such as arsons. If necessary, plan the action with a few (highly trusted) people but only have one or two people actually carry out the action. Do not leave out important positions but use only as many people as necessary.

-In addition to the people who directly carry out an action, some positions that might be necessary include someone with an emergency phone number, lookouts, someone to monitor local law enforcement radio channels, drivers, navigators, photographers or video recorders, people to distract cops and security guards, and people to help get activists released if anyone is arrested. Some activists may be able to fill multiple positions.

-Only use drivers who are not involved in the action if absolutely necessary. You do not want to have to wait to get picked up if something goes wrong and you have to leave early.

40

-Progress as a group. If you are an expert at raiding laboratories when you recruit a new cellmate, do not make him/her raid a laboratory right away. Do something easy and low-risk with him/her first. Remember that you were once inexperienced, too.

-Respect your cellmates. If someone only wants to liberate, graffiti, and glue locks, but wants to avoid arson because of heavier charges, respect that. You are all doing infinitely more than most humans and you are all heroes. In many cases, it is also tactically ideal to avoid arson in case you get caught and imprisoned, preventing future activism.

-Fur farm liberations should be carried out from June through September. Earlier and the animals may be too young and die. Later and it may be too late to save them.

-If releasing animals into the wild, do research ahead of time to ensure that the species you are releasing can survive in the area you are releasing them into.

-If you liberate animals who cannot be released into the wild, you might need two teams. The first team will get the animals out of the building, then the second team will come with vehicles. The first team can go back and destroy stuff or leave with the second team. The second team has to get out right away to ensure that the animals get out.

-If you liberate animals who cannot be released into the wild (due to species and location or experimental implants), arrange a safe house or sanctuary for the liberated animals before taking action.

-If you liberate animals who will need veterinary care, arrange for a veterinarian to treat the animals before taking action.

-The owner of the safe house or sanctuary and the veterinarian should be very trusted people who support direct action but are not involved in direct action or any other illegal activities. Do not tell these people any unnecessary details about the action. Do not tell them what specific laboratory or farm you are going to raid, who you are going to take action with, or when you are going to raid it. Only tell them what species of animals will be liberated, how many will be liberated, their ages, information on experimental implants, when they will arrive at the person's house, and any other information relevant to caring for the animals. These people need to adhere to a strict security culture as much as the activists do. Not doing so will get the activists arrested and get the animals a death sentence.

-If you raid a fur farm that is surrounded by a fence and you are unable to get the animals out of the fence, cut as many holes as possible and open the gates to allow for a maximum number to escape.

-If you raid a fur farm and are unable to release some or all of the animals, you will do a lot of good if you destroy the breeding cards. This costs fur farms a lot of money and can even cause them to shut down. If you are able to release some of the animals but not all of them, release as many of the breeding animals as possible. You can cover animals who you are unable to release in non-toxic die. They will still be murdered but the farmer will lose money.

-Laboratory raids are one of the most dangerous and complex actions you can take. Do not carry out a laboratory raid until you have a lot of experience with direct action. The most important part of a laboratory raid is making as secure of a plan as possible which means putting a lot of time into researching the laboratory's security systems, blueprints, and other helpful information and spending a lot of time revising the plan.

-Before raiding a laboratory, read this (http://www.nocompromise.org/issues/15shad_act.html).

-If you raid a laboratory, do as much damage as you can. Confiscating or destroying data and destroying equipment will cause the laboratory to lose a lot of money. Be careful to not accidentally destroy research that is unrelated to animal testing or possessions of professors who are not involved in animal testing.

-If you raid a laboratory, some things to keep in mind (from The Animal Liberation Primer) include:

1) Knowledge of the building noting all security, exits, stairways, doors, and of course, the location of the laboratory.
2) Knowledge of the number and species of animals, and the physical condition that they are in depending on the experiments they are being used for.
3) Ways to bypass locks and doors (i.e. lock picks, drilling equipment, crowbars, sledgehammers, etc.).
4) A way to bypass security systems and guards if they exist.
5) Lookouts with walkie talkies and preferably also police scanners to monitor police activity.
6) Boxes or animal carriers to safely transport the animals in.
7) Dependable vehicles to take animals away.
8) A very trusted and competent veterinarian to examine and treat the animals after they have been liberated.
9) Safe, caring, and dedicated homes for all the animals.
10) A brilliant plan to bring all these together.

-If you paint a message, do so on brick, wood, or metal. Glass is easy to clean.

-If you paint a message, make sure that you spell everything correctly. Use a dictionary if necessary. Make sure that you do not run out of room.

-Excess paint can be poured on the building's floor or outside of the door.

-Make sure to not get paint on your clothes or shoes.

-If you use spraypaint, mount a plastic pistol-grip handle on the can to ensure that the paint sprays in the direction of the target and not towards you.

-Paint bombs can be made by filling Christmas tree ornaments or balloons with paint.

-Paint-filled squirt guns can be used in place of paint bombs. Bring a plastic bag and rubber band to prevent paint from dripping after use.

-If you glue locks, include cut up paperclips for added effectiveness. Make sure to glue all of the locks on the target building or vehicle. Use a glue tube with a pointed tip.

-If you destroy windows, painting them with glass etching fluid (hydrofluoric acid) is much quieter than smashing them. This can be purchased at craft stores. Alternatively, you can mix ammonium bifluoride with sulfuric acid. The solution will corrode glass after reacting with water which will happen when the windows are washed.

-If you have to smash windows, you can use a slingshot or BB gun if the glass is too thick to be penetrated by a thrown rock.

-If you slash tires, stab their sidewalls. This prevents them from being repaired.

-If you do multiple things at once, do the loudest things last (smashing windows and slashing tires), then run. Slashing tires is loud.

-Vehicles can be damaged and destroyed by painting them, covering them with paint stripper or break fluid, gluing locks, slashing tires, smashing windows, covering windows with etching fluid, putting sand or oil in petrol/gasoline tanks, putting sand in oil reserves, cutting belts/wires/hoses, and firebombing.

-If you paint messages, destroy windows with glass etching fluid, or use paint stripper, bring a plastic bag for the used paint brushes and cans.

-Before carrying out arson, firebombing, or bombing, go inside the targeted building or vehicle to ensure that there are no non-human animals or non-target humans inside.

-Do not bring tools that could be considered weapons unless it is necessary in order to avoid being charged with being an 'armed criminal'. Only use a BB gun or slingshot if the glass is too thick to break with a brick. Only use a Molotov cocktail if a jug of kerosene will not be as effective. Only bring BBs to slow down pursuers if you will be in a hallway or somewhere else that they will be very effective.

Planning The Action

Before even planning an action, make sure that everything will be
taken care of if you are arrested. If you or your cellmates have
companion animals ('pets') or small children, make sure that there

is someone who will be able to take care of them if you are arrested. This does not mean telling someone that you are going to take direct action and this does not mean making any plans ahead of time. This does mean deciding on a few people who you will talk to if you are arrested. These should be people who are not involved in direct action, not at risk of arrest themselves, and preferably not heavily involved in the Liberation movement. These people should have keys to your house or know where a hidden key is. They should have a list of people who will need to be called including family and friends, your employer, your lawyer, and someone to put up bail money. This person should know where computers, cell phones, and other electronic devices, as well as militant literature, weapons, and other incriminating evidence are kept in your home or vehicle so that they can be removed before the police come to search. Have a few people ready to perform each of these tasks in case you cannot get a hold of one or two of them. Memorize each of their phone numbers. Decide on a code word or phrase that will be used if they need to go to your house to remove items or make sure that they know that that is part of their job if you get arrested. If you call from the police station, you do not want the police to overhear you telling them to remove incriminating evidence from your home.

-If you or any of your cellmates cannot afford bail or lawyers, decide ahead of time who will pay if any of you are arrested.

-Do all planning in real life. Do not talk about direct action in or near the home or vehicle of yourself or another activist. Do not have any cell phones or other electronic devices near you. Make sure that no one else has a cell phone or other electronic device. Be outside in the country far from anything human-made.

-Never use the same location twice. If you are always at the same place and the government suspects you, they might put a device in that area (way too small and well-hidden for you to detect) that will record what you say. Do not put it past them to find out where you meet and plan even if it is far out of town and far from your home. It is better to be over-cautious than imprisoned.

-Everyone directly involved in the action should be present for every planning meeting. People who are not directly involved, including people who are indirectly involved such as people with safe houses and veterinarians, should not be present.

-Everyone involved in the action should be made aware of all risks involved, including the risk of infiltrators and traitors and the risk of imprisonment, and be willing to take these risks. Everyone should know what to do to minimize all risks and everyone should reach a consensus on the cell's security policy. Take time to ensure that everyone understands the importance of security culture.

-Do a lot of planning. If you do not carry out your first action until a few months after forming your cell, that's fine. Give yourselves time to prepare yourselves and construct as good of a plan as possible.

-Make your plan as foolproof and secure as possible, but do not think that it is perfect. There is always some amount of risk of getting caught.

-The plan should include everything from meeting up before the action until people leave for home after the action. The plan should include everything discussed in this guide and anything else that is necessary in keeping you secure and effective.

-As you formulate and finalize your plan, think about how you can beat the system. This can be something really obvious and easy such as wearing a ski mask to avoid security cameras or it can be something that is more challenging like disabling a laboratory's security cameras and alarms before taking action.

-Try to think like the murderers, cops, and agents think. Put yourself in their place. The murderers want to keep their identities and locations secret to avoid getting attention from activists. Cops and agents will use various tactics in attempt to arrest you even if they only have evidence of you doing legal activism.

-Read this (http://nocompromise.org/issues/08minkraid.html) direct

48

action account to get an idea of what a real action is like. Make sure that everyone you are taking action with reads this. Pay very close attention to every detail.

-Watch videos of direct action (search 'ALF' on YouTube) to see what it is really like. Many videos are made up primarily of action-packed clips of breaking into buildings and smashing things. Most direct actions, especially complex liberations, are not nearly this intense, but they require just as much planning and security. This (http://www.youtube.com/watch?v=VfCQQNVtEnI) video shows what a fur farm liberation is like. This (http://www.youtube.com/watch?v=0SirWRwVyHQ) video shows what a laboratory liberation is like. This (http://www.youtube.com/watch?v=cqZtJvSaFIQ) video contains lots of action-packed clips.

-Determine everyone's roles and determine if people will split up into smaller groups or pairs during the action.

-Determine any new skills that you and your cellmates will need, such as lock-picking, using crowbars or wire cutters, parkour, and anything else that might be necessary. Practice these skills. In the long term, you and your cellmates should learn skills that each other do not know. Have at least two people who know each important skill in case someone is not available for a particular action. This will prevent putting excess pressure on one person and ensure a balance of responsibility.

-Obtain and study road maps, photographs, and satellite images of your target and the surrounding area. Google Earth is a good resource. If raiding a laboratory, attempt to obtain blueprints. Be careful to not leave any evidence when obtaining information. Use a public computer out of view of security cameras and wipe the keyboard and mouse when you are done to remove fingerprints, or, if using your own computer, use Tor (https://www.torproject.org/) and a secure operating system such as Ubuntu (http://www.ubuntu.com/). Burn all data from your research before taking action in case your house or vehicle is raided and because printed pages have the printer's serial number embedded.

-Find out the hours that your target is open and make sure that no one will be there when you take action. Keep in mind there may be janitors or security guards during off-hours. Fur farmers are known to have dogs and humans guarding their farms at night, especially during 'pelting season' (the time of year when the animals are murdered).

-Never use real names during an action. Assign each person a fake name to be used during the action. These can be regular human names, other names, letters, or numbers. New names should be assigned prior to each action. Be sure to remember your own name as well as those of everyone else.

-If any of your scouting missions are undercover, fake names should also be used for these. New names should be assigned prior to every scouting mission and prior to the action.

-If your action involves a lot of people, making it hard to remember fake names and hard to recognize people, you may want to tape a piece of paper with a number to each person's shirt, front and back. Make sure that everyone remembers their own number and that the papers will not fall off. Burn the papers and tape as soon after the action as possible.

-Make sure that everyone knows what radio channels will be used.

-Make sure that everyone knows any code words that may be used.

-You might want to set up an emergency phone number with a very trusted person in case things go wrong. This should be someone who is not involved in the action but can pick you up if you are on the run, if you get lost, or if things go wrong in any way. The phone should have call waiting so that activists can always get through and should be a cell phone rather than a landline. This person should be a good distance away from the location of the action. You or someone in your cell and the person with the emergency phone should have large detailed road maps in case you need to be picked up or get lost. If you have to call the emergency number, assume that the government is eavesdropping. Do not say anything related to the action. Only say as much as is necessary such as that you need to be picked up and what location you are at. Ensure that the person with the emergency number knows to not ask any unnecessary questions.

-Since cell phones should never be taken with while carrying out direct action, if you need to call the emergency number you will need to use a pay phone. Even if your plan does not involve splitting up, everyone in your cell should know the emergency number or have it written down in a zipper pocket and have change for a pay phone in case you are forced to scatter or someone gets lost. Never use the same pay phone twice, be cautious of security cameras and witnesses, and try to not leave sweat or fingerprints on the phone.

-Decide ahead of time who will bring what supplies.

-Determine how long each part of the action will take, what time to head towards the regroup location, and what time to arrive at the regroup location. Be as precise as possible. This is especially important if your plan involves splitting up or if the driver will not be involved in the action and will be meeting you to pick you up.

-Have a cover story ready in case you are pulled over while driving to or from the action or approached by a cop or anyone else while near the place of action.

-Make backup plans in case something goes wrong. Do you abandon the mission? Do you change tactics? Do you switch targets?

-Backup plans should be as detailed, secure, and well thought-out as primary plans.

-Determine how the decision to switch to a backup plan will be made, what circumstances might require such a decision, and how the decision will be communicated to others if the action involves splitting up. There is no time for democracy during direct action. If the leader says to switch to the backup plan, the decision should not be argued.

-Determine where people will regroup if you are forced to split up or scatter. This should be a fair distance away from action, preferably a mile or more.

-Find several escape routes and alternate regroup locations in case things go bad.

-You may want to assign a number to each regroup location or escape route so that if you have to scatter you can yell out that number so your cellmates know which location to regroup at. The leader should be the one to choose which location to regroup at to minimize confusion.

-Before finalizing plans, it may be beneficial to scout the place of action. If you have not done so yet, you can find escape routes and regroup locations during your scouting missions.

-After scouting, refine your plan and go through it many times with your cell and make sure that everyone knows exactly what they have to do. Make the final plan very detailed. Do not write it down or record it in any way.

-Make sure that everyone is comfortable with the plan and their role (make adjustments as necessary) and knows all of the details, including who will be bringing what supplies. It only takes one person to make one small error for the action go wrong and very possibly get your whole cell in prison.

-If anything at all falls through or if you get new information that interferes with your plan, postpone or call off the action. Do not risk arrest.

-Do not pressure people (whether or not they are already part of your cell or the Liberation underground) to take action if they are tired, sick, or stressed. Do not risk your freedom and security. Taking a temporary break from direct action will help you and your cell-mates to calm down, relax, and clear your minds, and leaving gaps between direct actions will reduce your chance of getting caught.

-If anyone feels unprepared or unsure or if there are any loose ends, take care of that, even if it means postponing or calling off the action.

-If anyone in your cell is sick, injured, recovering from sickness or injury, or even just tired or unalert, or could in any other way hinder the action, call it off. It is not worth the risk. Yes, you can save animals, but if you mess up and get caught now, you will not be able to save nearly as many in the future. Do not take any unnecessary risks.

-If the action or a scouting mission needs to be canceled at the last minute, you may be in a position where you cannot discuss the action (for example, in a vehicle). Decide before taking action or scouting what you will say to alert your cellmates that the action needs to be aborted and you need to turn around. If you are the driver, you do not want your cellmates to ask why you turn around. If you are not the driver, you need an inconspicuous way of alerting the driver. If you are near a building or vehicle, you need an inconspicuous way of alerting all of your cellmates.

-If plans fall through or if the action is called off or does not go according to plan, do not dwell on it and do not get mad at who you think is responsible. Underground activists say that most planned direct actions never happen because something comes up. Do not let it discourage you. Simply revise your plan or make a new one.

Scouting
In many cases, you should scout your target and the surrounding area after putting together a preliminary action plan. Scouting is especially important for liberations when taking time to scout on the

night of action means less time to liberate and less animals liberated.

-Do not bring a cell phone or other electronic device with you during scouting missions or the action and make sure that no one else does. Make sure that there are no cell phones or other electronic devices in the vehicle if you use one.

-Do not cut holes in fences or do anything else that leaves behind evidence during scouting missions. Doing so will put the area under very heavy surveillance for a long time.

-Do not leave behind sweat, hair, or anything else containing DNA.

-Have a cover story ready in case you are approached by cops or anyone else.

-Do the first scouting mission during the day to get oriented and learn the layout of the area. Some of the things that should be done during the daylight scouting mission include:
--Look for security cameras, alarms, trip wires, motion-sensor spotlights, other security devices, and other potential obstacles.
--Look for drop-off and pick-up locations if you have designated driver(s).
--Look for places relatively far away from the target for the driver to park or circular routes for the driver to take while the action is carried out.
--Look for alternate driving routes in case there is road construction.
--Make sure that there is room to turn around in drop-off, pick-up, and parking locations. Avoid fields because your vehicle could get stuck. Avoid soft ground because your vehicle will leave incriminating tire tracks. Avoid dead-end roads where other vehicles could block you in. Avoid areas with security cameras. Parking locations should be at least a mile from the target for high-risk actions and closer for lower-risk actions.
--Look for entrance and exit points to your target.
--Look for a primary walking route and regroup location. Regroup locations should not be in busy areas or financial districts.

--Look for several alternate escape routes and regroup in case you are seen by cops or other witnesses. Backup regroup locations should be about a mile away from the place of action. Make sure that escape are not very obvious so that cops will have a hard time pursuing you to your regroup location. If everyone in your cell is good at parkour, you may want to intentionally involve obstacles such as fences in your escape routes.

--If you have a parking or pick-up location that is far from your target, the regroup location should be closer so that you can meet up at the regroup location and walk to the vehicle together.

--Look for dark, inconspicuous hiding spots along the routes to and from the place of action and along escape routes in case you are chased.

--Look for dumpsters in case you need to dump supplies. These should only be used if necessary because supplies should be washed and tools should be filed before being dumped. If possible, do not dump multiple things in the same dumpster.

--Make sure that there are no security cameras near drop-off and pick-p locations, near the parking location, along escape routes, near where you will be entering and exiting the target area, or near regroup locations. Escape routes and driving routes should not go through busy areas.

--Look for potential obstacles and determine what tools will be needed.

--If you will be using walkie talkies, ensure that they will work in the area you are taking action.

-If your action will take place at night (which it should), an additional scouting mission should be done at the time of night during whichh the action will take place. This should be done on the same night of the week as when the action will take place. The purpose of the night scouting mission(s) is:

--Watch for police patrols, security guards, and other potential witnesses. If there are patrols or guards at this time, take action at a different time of night or on a different night of the week. This applies to your primary walking route and regroup location, escape routes and regroup locations, driving routes, and pick-up, drop-off, and parking locations.

--Look for lights that will be on near your drop-off, pick--up, and parking locations, along escape routes, and at re-group locations. If necessary, revise these details of the plan.

-Scout your primary walking route and escape routes when you scout the rest of the area. This should be done several times during a daylight scouting mission and again during a night scouting mission.

-Do not wear your underground gear while scouting, especially during the daytime scouting mission(s). Put on normal walk-ing/jogging gear and do not let yourself look too suspi-cious. Do not continually drive or walk past. Make a jog-ging route. Scouting with one other person and acting like you are dating makes for a good cover story in some situations.

-If there are not a lot of people around during your night scouting missions, you may be able to avoid being seen. If this is possible, wear a mask and take all of the security precautions that you will take during the action.

-If possible, do not let anyone see you when scouting. Hide in a ditch or bushes whenever you hear a vehicle. However, if you think that you were seen and you are not wearing underground gear, you may not want to hide because it will look suspicious. Make judgments on a case-by-case basis.

-Be very cautious when scouting, do not scout more times than necessary, and do not look suspicious. Activists have been arres-ted because they were seen acting suspicious near their target prior to the action.

-Do most or all daylight scouting missions a long time before the action. Do a night scouting mission one week prior to the action. You may also want to do a night scouting mission one day prior to the action.

-Do further scouts if you feel at all unprepared but scout as few times as possible to avoid raising suspicion.

-For more detailed scouting instructions and tips, read this (http://www.animalliberationfront.com/ALFront/Activist%20Tips /Security/Scouting.htm).

Before The Action
Do not contact a company prior to an action regarding their cruelty to animals (or for any other reason). The action should be above-ground or underground, not both.

-Do not act suspiciously happy, excited, or nervous in the days preceding the action.

-Do not go to Animal Liberation, Earth Liberation, or direct action websites more often than usual in the days preceding the action and try to avoid opening direct action guides. If you have to open something, use Tor (https://www.torproject.org/) and a secure operating system such as Ubuntu (http://www.ubuntu.com/).

-Go over the plan with everyone involved multiple times in a secure location. Work out any potential flaws such as security concerns.

-Do not use any type of drugs, including alcohol. You need to be fully alert.

-Get plenty of sleep. You will not get much, if any, sleep on the night of action until you you get home and you need to be fully alert.

-Eat plenty of food and drink plenty of water.

-Make sure that your gear fits tightly.

-Wash your clothes and tools immediately before the action. Be aware of things like batteries in flashlights that may have fingerprints. You do not want any hair falling off of your clothes and you do not want DNA from your gloves being left at the place of action if you sweated last time you wore them. Immediately after washing your tools, ensure that they do not have any hair or other evidence on them and put them in a plastic bag. Keep them in the bag until you use them and put them back in the bag immediately afterwards. This will keep them free of fingerprints and DNA so that, if necessary, you can dump them in a dumpster. Make sure that the plastic bag does not have fingerprints or DNA on it. One liberationist was convicted because of fingerprints on a burnt paint can, demonstrating that it is very important to keep all equipment free of fingerprints and DNA.

-Before leaving home, make sure that you do not have anything in your home or vehicle(s) that you do not want cops or agents to see. Keep them at a friend's house if possible. This includes maps, plans (it is a very bad idea to write down plans), militant literature including direct action guides, diaries, address books, drugs (activists should not use drugs anyway), weapons, money, credit cards, and other valuables.

-If driving to the place of action, remove any unnecessary objects from your vehicle before leaving home. If something falls out where you park, it could be used against you.

-Before leaving home, double check that you have all clothing, tools, maps, and other supplies that will be needed.

-If you use a vehicle, make sure that your petrol/gasoline tank is full. Make sure that your headlights, taillights, and turn signals work. Not using them would give cops a reason to pull you over. Use a vehicle without bumper stickers.

-Immediately before leaving home, check your clothes, shoes, gear, and vehicle for tracking devices and bugs. Manually search and, if possible, use a radio frequency detector.

-Do not be late to meeting up with your cellmates. Timing is important because the ideal time of night to take direct action only spans a few hours (approximately 2:00am-4:00am). The meetup location should be a neutral, public location rather than an activist's house. It should also be an area that is not crowded.

-If you drive to the place of action, do not talk about anything, even things unrelated to direct action, while in the vehicle. If there is a bug in your vehicle, you do not want the government to hear the voices of everyone involved in the action.

The Action

This is not a game. One small mistake and you and your friends could face years in prison. Do not take direct action lightly. When taking action, adhere strictly to the plan as much as possible. Follow all decided-upon procedures such as staying in sight or earshot of cellmates or keeping walkie talkies turned on, not talking during the action unless absolutely necessary, keeping track of time to make sure that you get to the regroup location in time, and all other parts of the plan.

-Do not bring a cell phone or other electronic device. Make sure that none of your cellmates bring a cell phone or other electronic device. Make sure that there are no cell phones or other electronic devices in your vehicle. Leave them at home.

-If you have to call off the action while you are on your way to the place of action, do not talk about the action while in a vehicle or any location where you could be overheard. Do not say that the action is being called off. Just turn around and tell your cellmates why later. Talk about this possibility while planning the action so that no one will get confused and ask suspicious questions if the driver takes a wrong turn or turns around.

-Make sure that you are not being followed by cops or agents when you drive to and from the action. If you are being followed, call off the action. If you go to prison, you cannot help animals or Earth for a long time.

-Do not park, or even drive, near the place of action, during scouting missions or during the action. The government can and has put tracking devices on activists' vehicles.

-Be careful about where you park, be out of view of security cameras, and make sure that security cameras and people do not see you get out of your vehicle carrying gear or a backpack. This applies to the action and to scouting missions.

-If time permits, turn off all vehicle lights, flashlights, and other lights and wait for about twenty minutes to get your eyes used to the dark. Alternatively, turn off all vehicle lights twenty minutes prior to getting to the parking location or being dropped off.

-If you bring water bottles or food, leave them inside of the vehicle.

-Lock your vehicle's doors.

-Leave the keys hidden somewhere near the vehicle. If one person has the keys and gets caught, everyone is stuck.

-You may want to cover your license plate while you are parked in case you are pursued by any angry farmer and have to drive away quickly. As long as no one is watching, uncover it before leaving so that you are not pulled over.

-Do not let security cameras or witnesses see you with your mask off and do not let security cameras see what vehicle you drive. Be careful where you park and do not make it too close to the place of action.

-Do not let security cameras or witnesses see you wearing or carrying your black clothes or backpack when getting out of your vehicle.

-Do not put your gear on until you have left your vehicle and put it on in a location where you will not be seen by witnesses or security cameras.

-Tie your shoes tightly so that you do not trip on laces and you have good support. This will be especially important if you need to run. If you wear a hat (which is usually a bad idea), make sure that it will not fall off. Make sure that your hood will not fall down if it is covering a headlamp. Keep your backpack zipped all the way. If you have any tools in your pockets, put them in zipper pockets and keep your pockets zipped.

-Keep your mask and gloves on at all times. There are hidden security cameras at almost all potential targets, even farms, and forensics are one of the main ways that activists are identified. Be careful that your mask does not get snagged on any equipment, fence, or branch and get pulled off.

-If you have a police scanner, double check that it is set to monitor the correct frequencies. Only put the earphone on one ear so that you can hear what is going on around you.

-When walking between your vehicle and the place of action, do not walk along roads. Walk through fields and avoid walking near houses. Hunch over and let your arms hang down so that, if anyone is watching, you do not look like humans.

-If possible, avoid walking through mud. Do not let mud, dirt, grass, or anything else get in your vehicle. Have plastic bags ready to put shoes and other dirty clothing and equipment in.

-While taking action, focus only on the action. Do not think about what could happen if you get caught, just know that getting caught is not an option. Be as efficient and effective as possible, and if anything goes wrong, stay calm and do not panic.

-Do everything at once. Your target will be under heavy surveillance for a long time after the action.

-Be time-efficient. The ideal time of night to take direct action only spans a few hours (approximately 2:00am-4:00am). Do not allow time for people to see you and call the cops and for the cops to arrive. Liberate animals as quickly as possible in order to liberate as many as you can.

-Watch for security cameras, alarms, trip wires, and other security devices. This should be done while scouting, but keep watch for them during the action in case you missed something.

-Do not walk near security cameras. Do not look at them. Do not let them see your eyes or the distance between your eyes. If possible, do not let them see you walking at all because gate recognition is used to identify people. Walk differently than you normally do.

-If you use a camera and/or camcorder (which is discouraged), do not let it be caught on security cameras. It can be used to identify you. If you use more than one device, do not release any photos or videos in which another camera or camcorder is visible. If you can afford it, buy a camera specifically for the action and dispose of it after the action.

-Do not talk during the action unless absolutely necessary. Security cameras and witnesses can hear your voice. If you have to talk, do not use the same slang or unique words that you usually do, disguise your voice, and do not call people by their real names. Use the fake names which were chosen during the planning stage.

-Always be watching for farmers, cops, witnesses, and vehicles.

-If you see a farmer, do not confront him/her, just run. Many farmers have guns and it is rumored that some fur farmers walk their property at night with guns looking for activists. Do not let this deter you from taking action, just make sure to not panic and leave the area quickly if you see anyone.

-There may be dogs or humans guarding your target. Have dog

treats and money ready to bribe them before approaching the target.

-Do not point your headlamp or flashlight towards houses, vehicles, towns, or roads. Cover it with a red screen. This makes it barely visible from a distance.

-Fur farmers, and probably other animal abusers, put aluminum on top of their fences so that if activists climb the fences they will make noise and attract attention. If fences are in your way, do not climb them. Use wire cutters to cut a hole and crawl through. If you have to cut through a chain or padlock, use bolt cutters or a lock pick.

-Before taking action at a farm, or even scouting if the scouting mission involves going onto the farmer's property, cross the perimeter of the property and go into a shed. Retreat quickly, be ready to run, and wait to see if anything happens. Even if nothing happens immediately, it may trigger an alarm that will alert the farm owner so you should wait for at least a few minutes. If nothing happens, go back in and scout or liberate, but always keep watch for farmers.

-The front door is rarely the best way in. Doors are usually locked and there might be alarms in the doorway. You might be able to enter through the roof or a wall. If your target is a shed or barn, you might be able to remove wall panels. Some fur farm sheds do not even have solid walls so you might be able to climb in under the cages. If your target is a laboratory, you might be able to climb in through windows.

-There may be alarms in doorways to fur farm sheds and/or on the perimeter of the farm or the farmer's property. Photoelectric sensors are placed at the corners of farms and create invisible fields. The fields can sometimes be ducked or rolled under.

-If the doors are locked and you have no other way in, you can pry the door off of its hinges with a crowbar, smash it in with a sledgehammer, pick the lock, or drill the lock.

-Cutting power can be effective against alarms because backup generators power essential things such as lighting and electronic gates and not necessarily alarm systems. Many power companies run tests when power goes out before alerting the owner of the property. This can give you a short opportunity to carry out a swift action. This may be only ten minutes or less. There are many types of alarm systems and this method will not always work or it may not give you enough time, so it is important to become familiar with your target's alarm systems and other security measures.

-If you are taking action inside of a laboratory or other building, peak around corners before you enter or pass by a room or hallway. Even if you think that you are the only ones in the building, do not take unnecessary risks. Caution is key.

-If you see someone, abandon the mission. It is not worth getting caught to save a few animals when that means that you cannot save more in the future.

-You may not want paint the ALF logo or in any way affiliate yourself with any existing group. If you are caught, you will have a longer prison sentence and heavier fines simply because you are part of a 'terrorist organization'.

-If liberating animals, be prepared for the animals to make a lot of noise and do not be scared away by the noise. According to a mink liberator with first-hand experience, '...what is deafening inside a shed is almost inaudible just 25 yards away.' This does not mean that the noise does not present any risk so you should attempt to target farms at which the sheds are not very close to a house.

-If an animal who you are liberating bites or scratches you, be forgiving. Obviously, the animals who are in laboratories, fur farms, and other places of abuse have every right to hate and fear humans. If you are going to be liberating animals, wear gloves that cannot be penetrated by teeth or claws so that you do not leave blood.

-Do not pet, feed, talk to, or otherwise comfort or interact with animals while liberating them. It is too dangerous. It is a waste of valuable time and if you talk to them your voice can be heard on security devices.

-Be extremely careful to not leave any physical evidence such as a used spraypaint can or tools with your fingerprints or vehicle/ house keys. These things can be, and have been, used to prosecute activists. Keys were the main piece of evidence used in the prosecution of two ALF activists and a burnt paint can with fingerprints was the main piece of evidence used against another.

-If you have a cut, scab, or other injury, make sure that you do not get blood on anything. It can be traced to you. Be very careful to not get cut on branches, fences, or equipment during the action. If blood does get on anything, remove it as well as you can.

-One activist was implicated by saliva found at the place of action. If you cough or sneeze, cover your mouth and nose with your arm.

-If possible, plant false evidence. Leave hair or anything else that you can think of found somewhere far from your home and far from the place of action.

-After the action, regroup if the action involved splitting up. Make sure that everyone is there, try to find anyone who is missing, and if possible, destroy incriminating evidence such as clothing. Wipe your shoes on the ground to remove as much evidence as possible. Remove seeds, leaves, and anything else stuck to your clothing. If you got cut or scratched during the action, do your best to clean it. Do not stay at the regroup location for any longer than necessary.

-If you run out of time and cannot finish the action and are out of range and unable to contact your cellmates, the action will have to go unfinished. Being late to the regroup location is too much of a security risk.

-If things go wrong during the action and you have to run, you may want to try to stick together, but not if it means wasting time finding each other or regrouping. In some situations, you may want to scatter to get rid of whoever is pursuing you, but try to at least stay in pairs of two. Pairs should be decided upon before the action to reduce confusion during the action. Focus on where you are running to because it is easy to get disoriented, change direction as you run, and waste time or get lost, especially at night. Decide before the action where you will run to if you get split up. Study maps and walk potential escape routes ahead of time so that you know exactly where to run to.

-If you cannot get to the regroup location, run as fast and far as you can. Get out of the area. Get rid of your clothes and tools (in separate dumpsters if possible). If you have an emergency number, call it.

-If you get hurt while running from police (for example, twist an ankle) ignore the pain and keep running fast and hard. You are Vegan and you are strong. A little pain is nothing compared to getting caught and going to prison.

-If you are seen and have to run, do not panic. With a clear mind and determination to not get caught, you will get out of it.

-If you get split up and are unable to regroup, do not call each other as soon as you get home. You will want to know if your friends escaped but calling right away would look very suspicious. When you do call, act like you are just calling to chat. Avoid saying things like 'Are you alright?' or 'That was close!'. It is too suspicious. Do not call anyone or answer any phone calls until you are calm because a shaky voice is suspicious.

After The Action

Do not lighten up on security just because an action is over. Some investigations last for years.

-If you drive from the place of action, do not talk about anything, even things unrelated to direct action, while in the vehicle. If there is a bug in your vehicle, you do not want the government to hear the voices of everyone involved in the action.

-Take a shower as soon as you get home to remove evidence such as soil residue.

-If any soil or grass or anything else was tracked into your vehicle, clean your vehicle as soon as you get home.

-Clothing and tools will have traces from the 'crime' scene. Fiber from your clothing left at the place of action can be traced. Soil, plant, and insect residue on clothing and equipment, especially shoes, is analyzed by crime scene analysts. Burn what you can at a campsite far from your home and far from the place of action. Do not burn anything at your home.

-Wash tools and anything else that is not burnable as soon as you get home to remove fingerprints and evidence from the place of action such as soil. Put everything in plastic bags before disposing of it. These should not be the same bags that clothing and equipment were placed in immediately after the action because those bags will contain evidence from the place of action such as soil and they may have fingerprints. Those bags should be burned.

-Tools leave unique marks. File their tips immediately after the ac tion. If a tool is used for more than one action (which is strongly discouraged), it should be filed immediately after each action.

-Things that cannot be burned should be disposed of in public dumpsters far from your home and far from the place of action. Put everything in separate dumpsters. Objects found in dumpsters have been used against activists.

-If you are unable to burn and dispose of things immediately after the action, wash them immediately and burn them as soon as possible.

-The most important things to burn or dispose of are shoes, backpacks, tools, and other unique items as opposed to more basic things like hoodies and sweatpants, but everything should be disposed of if possible. It is not worth the risk just to save a little money.

-Make sure that you are not seen by witnesses or security cameras when burning and disposing of supplies. Consider doing so late at night while wearing a dark hoodie and a hat.

-Optionally give clothing and tools to someone who is trustworthy but not involved in the action to dispose of them.

-Do not keep any souvenirs. This includes anything from the place of action or clothing or tools you used. What you did is important, not what you used, and souvenirs are a major security risk.

-Do not return to the place of action to see your success. It is way too suspicious. Many criminals have been caught this way.

-Avoid passing by the place of action after the action. If you have to pass by it, do not do anything suspicious like slowing down or even smiling as you pass.

-Debrief. Do this within a few days of the action so that you do not forget anything. Discuss what went well and what did not go well including planning, execution, and anything else. Talk about what was the most challenging part of the action, what mistakes were made, and what can be done to make future actions more secure, efficient, and effective. Be honest about mistakes that were made but be polite when pointing out mistakes that others made. Everyone makes mistakes and the mistakes should be learned from, not used to embarrass people. Remind everyone to maintain a strict security culture. The debrief meeting is the last time that the action should ever be discussed with the exception of writing a communique if that has not yet been done. Make sure that you are talking in a secure location with no phones or other electronic devices nearby. Be outside in the country far from buildings, vehicles, and other human-made objects. Security at the debrief meeting is just as important as security at the planning meetings.

-Do not act suspiciously happy, excited, or nervous in the days following the action.

-Do not go to Animal Liberation, Earth Liberation, or direct action websites more often than usual in the days following the action.

-If you read your own communique, do not do anything to give yourself away, especially if you have a webcam (many computers have built-in webcams) or microphone. Webcams can be hacked and computers can be tapped. If you smile or laugh while reading your cell's communique, you might give yourself away. Do not check Bite Back and NAALPO more frequently than usual after taking action.

Avoiding Capture
-Think about how and when you could get caught. You could get caught before the action, either because your planning is over-heard or because you get seen by security cameras or witnesses.

-Do not give the police any reason to pull you over. They are much more likely to pull people over at night. Use a vehicle with no bumper stickers.

-Bring your driver's license, proof of insurance, and any other required documents in case you are pulled over, but leave these, along with maps, water bottles, and food, in the vehicle when taking action.

-Put bolt cutters and other supplies under the seats, under blankets, or in the trunk before you leave because if you are pulled over you might not have time to hide them.

-Do not speed. Drive at least several miles per hour under the speed limit at all times and watch for reduced speed zones.

-Make sure that your license plates are current.

-Make sure that your headlights, taillights, break lights, hazard lights, and turn signals work. Use your turn signals.

-Wear your seatbelt.

-Have a cover story ready in case you are pulled over. If you are pulled over, do not panic or do anything suspicious. Be friendly and polite to the officer, but not to the point of seeming suspicious. If you are pulled over and for any reason get out of your vehicle, close the door behind you. Not doing so might be legal grounds for a vehicle search.

-Another danger is your vehicle being seen by security cameras or witnesses. Do not make any stops along the way unless absolutely necessary. Most petrol/gasoline stations have security cameras. Make sure that you are not being followed by cops or agents. They may be using unmarked vehicles and will oftentimes be in groups of two or three vehicles. Use side roads and make lots of turns in order to minimize witnesses. Avoid major roads and financial districts.

-Do not drive or park very close to the place of action; it is too suspicious. If possible, park a few miles away and walk, but re- member that it will take time walking, especially while carrying tools and backpacks, so get there plenty early.

-Your vehicle could be seen by security cameras or witnesses, and the government puts tracking devices on activists' vehicles. Even if you use a radio frequency detector and GPS blocker, you can- not be positive that your technology is good enough to detect and neutralize theirs. Park out of view of security cameras.

-Park on hard ground that will not retain tire tracks. You cannot be seen or caught on any security cameras near your target without your clothes on.

-Make sure that you are in a secure location when you get dressed and undressed. Do not get dressed until as late as possible because you will look very suspicious with a mask on if there are any witnesses nearby.

-If you get pulled over by the police, you do not want to be wearing a ski mask or even solid black clothing.

-If you are seen by a security camera or witness getting out of your vehicle wearing or carrying a mask and dark clothes, or if your vehicle is seen near the place of action, you can be identified. You could get caught during the action. This could be by security cameras or witnesses seeing you during the action. You could leave behind evidence which will later be used against you. For example, if you have keys in your pocket (which is strongly discouraged), they might fall out.

-If you forget to take off jewelry before the action, it might fall off. If you leave behind a spraypaint can, tool, glove, or any other equipment or clothing at the place of action, it can be traced if you left any fingerprints or sweat on it.

-Only bring what is necessary, leave your keys hidden near your vehicle, and make sure to not leave anything behind. Fingerprints, blood, saliva, hair, carpet fibers, footprints, tire tracks, and secu-

rity camera images and voice recordings are all potential security threats.

-You could get caught after the action. Similar to before the action, you could get caught taking off your clothes or getting into your vehicle. Take off clothes as soon as possible so that you have less of a chance being seen in them, but make sure that there are no people or security cameras around when you undress.

-Put everything under seats or in the trunk. You could be caught if your clothing or equipment is found in your house or vehicle.

-Do not speed or give the police any other reason to pull you over.

-Do not leave your gear lying in the open. Until you can dispose of and burn tools and equipment, keep them in inconspicuous locations. Keep your hoodie and ski mask with other winter clothing. Keep your bolt cutters with other tools. If you need to buy extra tools so that it is not suspicious just having bolt cutters and a sledgehammer, do it. If you need to buy extra ski clothes, do it. It is better to spend a little bit of money than to go to prison.

-You could be caught talking about or reporting the action. Never talk about an action after it has taken place and be extremely cautious if you report your action to Bite Back or NAALPO. The government is good at hacking, tapping, and tracing. You could be caught by a snitch or infiltrator.

-If you have to talk about past actions, do so outside with no electronic devices nearby and check whoever you are talking to for a wire or other sound recording device.

-Be very careful about who you take action with.

From the Animal Liberation Front
A few ways people get caught include:

Physical Evidence
Diaries, plans, manuals, stuff left at the action by accident or on purpose, communiques, stored information on computers and paper trails from the use of bank cards and the hire or purchase of equipment. Avoid these by always paying cash and destroying or removing everything relating to the action before you go on it. Do not take anything traceable to you (like ID or engraved jewelery) on actions. Consider using false ID if you are hiring gear. If you must use a computer encrypt all files with PGP.

Forensic Evidence
Mainly just fingerprints and DNA, but also includes matching up of tool usage, soil samples and footprints. Watch out for prints on things that are not immediately obvious like flashlight batteries. Ensure everything is fingerprint free before the action and wear gloves and hats. Dispose of traceable items like clothes and tools as soon as possible post-action.

Witnesses
People being able to identify you or your vehicle, not just at the action, but also on the way there, or even just leaving your house at a connected time. Includes images from CCTV or police video/stills teams. Plan meet-ups, routes to the action, etc. avoiding cameras and nosy neighbours. Disguise yourselves and wear indistinguishable clothes. Do not tell people what they do not need to know.

Surveillance
Includes phone taps, post and email interception, listening devices and following you or placing tracking units in your vehicles. Conducted by numerous, and sometimes competing, state and private agencies. Operates at various levels from the fairly routine, which should not effect your activity that much, through to ones where everything you say and do is listened to and watched. Avoid talking or communicating about anything action related in your home, over

email or on a phone. Look out for cops following you on actions.

Observing Protests
Think long and hard about attending protests if you are involved in direct action. Remember police frequently photograph and videotape demonstrations and sometimes detain or arrest activists just to get information, fingerprints and DNA samples from them.

-The animals would rather you stay safe and active instead of attending protests.

-A legal observer should be present at all protests. Their purpose is to record what the police do. If this is not an option, protesters should fill as much of the observer's role as possible.

-If the observer is a representative of a media outlet, the observer has a stronger legal foundation and is less vulnerable to police. Laws in some states prevent people from videotaping the audio part of an event. This law does not apply to media reporters.

-If the observer is a media representative, he/she should consider applying for a press pass which gives many privileges that normally would not be allowed.

-At large demonstrations, you might want several trained legal observers and even lawyers present.

-Observers should dress professionally. This makes them more credible and makes the police more cautious.

-Observers are more likely to be arrested than protesters. They should be free of drugs and weapons.

-If there are enough observers, they should work in teams of two.

-A legal observer should bring a video camera, clipboard, plastic bag in case it is raining, several pens, note paper, complaint forms, and if possible, a shirt that identifies the observer as such. If there are no observers, a protester should bring these things, camcord, and take notes.

-To maintain credibility, observers should not engage in protests, threats, insults, or anything else besides observing and recording.

-Observers should be as close to the action as possible.

-If approached by police or media, observers should be clear and direct that they are there as an observer only and do not want to speak to them.

-If the police approach you, ask for their card. If they refuse, ask for and write down their name, official title, address, and phone number. Write down the time, date, what happened, and the exact words spoken. This applies to observers and protesters. If you do not have a pen and paper, tell an observer about the encounter as soon as possible so that it can be written down.

-If the police are physically harming protesters, the observer should ask them politely to stop rather than physically stopping them, if possible.

-If an arrest is made, an observer should ask the arresting officer(s) for and write down their name, badge number, and supervising officer. This can be used against them if the arrest is illegal and it will make them less likely to make illegal arrests and less likely to be brutal in arrests.

-A checklist of things for observers to write down (from the Animal Liberation Front):
  --Names, badge numbers and other identifying characteristics of all cops and agents present. If they refuse to supply you with these, or if they are not visible, make note of these.
  --The manner in which the officers are identified. If there is no identification supplied, make note of this.

--Who is in charge. If they refuse to tell you who is in charge, make note of this.

--Warnings given, who gave them, time given.

--License numbers of private vehicles moving through the demonstrations.

--Name(s) of person(s) arrested. Also ask the person there birth date so you can track them.

--Any unusual circumstances, force used, injuries, sweeps.

--Witness names, address and phone numbers.

--Names of media present.

--Names of people with cameras.

--Always track time in your notes.

--Note other facts that seem important.

-Keep this information in a secure location. If the police break any laws and you press charges against them, it may not be until months afterward that you need the notes. Keep a copy and give a copy to a legal coordinator.

-Video cameras are one of the most effective tools to deter police brutality.

-Use a cheap camera. Police have been known to hit them with batons.

-Use a video camera with a light. Some of the worst police brutality occurs at night. If they see the light of a video camera, they are much less likely to use excessive force.

-Make sure that the police know they are being recorded. If your camera has a light and it is night, turn it on. The police avoid arresting people for trivial reasons if they know that they are being recorded.

-The police will commonly make arrests for things like jay-walking. Video recorders deter them from doing this because they do not want to be documented making such a trivial arrest.

-If it is a large protest and you can work with friends, have a runner (someone who gets tapes to a secure location as quickly as possible if police brutality is recorded so that the police cannot take the tape). Have a buddy who watches for nearby police, police activity that the observer misses, and anything else that the observer should be aware of. Have a reporter who can act as a witness or provide information to media.

-Bring several extra tapes in case you record an incident and your runner takes the tape.

-You might want to work with another recorder. One of you will go in close to the action and the other will hang back and watch the recorder who is closer in. This is for added security. There is also the option of two recorders on opposite sides of the protest watching out for each other and covering the protest more fully.

-Keep the camera on the whole time. Police will arrest people for things like standing on the curbs. These charges have often been dismissed because video footage proved that the person was not where the police claimed. It is also important to keep the camera on because gaps can be used to attack video footage.

-If the police are making an arrest, record the arrest. It is very important that the police know that you are recording them because this deters brutality. In one situation, cops were seen throwing a protester between them to make it seem as if the protester was resisting arrest. They will also circle their victim to make the arrest harder to record. They hate being recorded doing this things so make that sure they know you are there.

-If the police are circling someone, observers should get in as close as possible and/or hold the camera above their head and angle it down.

-If working with a lawyer, label your tapes 'Attorney work product, privileged and confidential'. This makes it harder for cops to use them.

-If the police are recorded doing something forceful or brutal, get the video footage aired. This will make the police much less likely to repeat the actions. Keep the original tape. Only give copies to the media because they might be friends with the police. Make sure that the tape only includes what you want aired. If you are paid for the tape, read the contract to make sure that they are not stopping you from showing it elsewhere.

Law Enforcement And Legal Rights
This section is written from a United States perspective. International laws vary. UK activists should refer to Free BEAGLES (http://www.freebeagles.org/).

-This section applies regardless of how much evidence the government has against you and regardless of whether you are suspected of or arrested for protesting, underground direct action, or anything else. This also applies whether or not you are responsible for what you are convicted of.

-Know your legal rights.

-Whether you are involved in legal activism or illegal direct action, you are at risk of being interrogated, being searched, having your house raided, having your vehicle searched, and being arrested. Do not leave things lying around your house or vehicle if you do not want them to be discovered. Know what to say if the police or FBI come to your house (with our without a warrant) or if you are approached or arrested.

-If you are approached by cops or agents and/or caught for illegal direct action, do not panic. Remain as calm as possible.

-Make sure that you have the mental ability to keep silent under intense pressure and threats. If you are threatened by cops or agents, it is most likely an empty threat.

-Do not believe anything that the police, FBI, or other government agents tell you. They will lie to you.

-You have the fifth amendment right to remain silent. You have this right even if you are detained or arrested. In some situations, if approached in public, you are legally required to provide your name, address, and/or date of birth. The laws on this vary by state. Only provide this information if asked for it and do not provide any other information. You are never required to provide your social security number or any other information. You are not required to provide any information if you are contacted at home.

-In some situations, you may be required to invoke your right to remain silent before exercising it. Before exercising your right to remain silent, say 'I invoke my fifth amendment right to remain silent. I do not wish to speak to the police/FBI.'

-Answer all questions with 'I have nothing to say. I want to talk to a lawyer.' or do not say anything at all. If they do not stop questioning you, say 'You are harassing me. Please leave me alone. I am going to talk to my lawyer.' Say this regardless of whether or not you have a lawyer.

-Do not say anything about friends and allies. Do not give names. Do not betray your friends, the movement, or the animals.

-If you are at a protest, do not tell cops or agents anything. They might ask what your name is, how long you have been protesting, who is in charge of the protest, or other seemingly harmless questions. They might be friendly or they might attempt to scare you into answering their questions. Say nothing.

-If you are approached in public by cops or agents, say 'Am I free to leave?' If you get any answer except for a definitive 'no', gather your things and walk or drive away without saying anything else.

-If you are told that you are not free to leave, say 'Am I being de-

80

tained?' If the answer is yes, ask what their probable cause is. Do not engage in conversation and do not answer any questions. If the answer is no, then you are under arrest. If you are arrested, cooperate with the arrest for your own safety and because by not doing so you could be charged with resisting arrest and/or assault on an officer. Do not engage in conversation and do not answer any questions. If you are not convicted of anything illegal, you may be able to sue the police.

-Cops have the right to pat you down to check for weapons but they do not have the right to a full search. If they attempt to search you without presenting a warrant, do not physically resist for your own safety and because you may be charged with assault on an officer. Say 'I do not consent to this search' and repeat this line until they stop. You may be able to sue them later.

-The only things you should ever say to cops or agents are the things outlined above. The only exception is if you witness a crime (a true crime such as theft or murder, not direct action) and are willing to help in an investigation. In this case, talk to a lawyer before helping the government to ensure that you are not tricked into providing information that can be used against you if you are ever investigated.

-Anything you say will be misquoted and used against you and other activists. If the FBI asks if you have heard of a mink liberation and you say 'I read about it in a newspaper' and they ask if you know anything about the ALF and you say 'I've heard of them', they will report 'Claims to know all about the ALF and is familiar with the recent mink liberation'.

-Do not tell them something just because they 'already know the answer'. If they already knew the answer, they wouldn't be asking you. Even if it is 'harmless' information, talking now means that they will suspect you if you stop talking later.

-Even if you do not say anything that they can manage to misquote and use against you, you are better off remaining silent. Which would you rather an FBI agent wrote in his log book: 'Spoke for 20 minutes to [your name]' or '[Your name] had nothing to say'?

-Lying to cops or agents is a federal offense. Saying something contradictory (such as 'no, I do not know anything about that raid' and 'yes, I read about it in the newspaper') out of fear or forgetfulness or clumsy wording is grounds for this. They might try to trick you into doing this.

-Do not try to outsmart them or trick them or lie to them. It is way too easy for even the most skilled people to get caught in a lie, accidental or intentional, and if you talk now but refuse to talk about your knowledge of an action later, this could be held against you. If you talk, you will talk your way into prison.

-If you are contacted by cops or agents at home, you do not have to provide any information, not even your name, address, or date of birth.

-If they call you, tell them that you have nothing to talk to them about, tell them to never call you again, and hang up.

-If they come to your house, say 'Am I being detained?' If they say no, say 'Am I under arrest?' If they say no, say 'Please leave me alone, you are harassing me.' If they do not leave, close and lock the door and ignore them.

-If they want to search your home or vehicle without a search warrant, do not let them. They will use social engineering in attempt to get you to let them search without a warrant. Just say no. If you say something like 'I'd rather you didn't' they will claim that you 'reluctantly consented to the search'. If they threaten to make a mess of your house if you make them come back with a warrant, stand your ground. They will make a mess of things either way.

-If they attempt to search your home or vehicle without presenting a warrant, do the same thing that you would do if they were to attempt to search you without presenting a warrant. Do not physically resist for your own safety and because you may be charged with assault. Say 'I do not consent to this search' and repeat this line until they leave. You may be able to sue them later.

-If they have a warrant, follow them and take notes of everything they do, including what they search through and what items they take, unless you are ordered not to.

-They might just wave a piece of paper. Demand to see the warrant. They legally have to let you read it. A warrant must be signed by a judge and specifically describe the place to be searched and items to be taken. A warrant looks like this (http://www.greenisthenewred.com/blog/wp-content/Images/100315_peter_young_raid_warrant_utah.pdf).

-If they raid your house or search your vehicle with a warrant but did not have a good reason to get the warrant, you may be able to sue them.

-Police and FBI are allowed to enter a house without a warrant if they witnessed the 'crime'.

-If a roommate or co-worker allows them to search your house or workplace, tell the cops or agents that you do not consent to the search and are going to contact an lawyer.

-The police and FBI are experts at social engineering. They will say various things in attempt to trick you, almost all of which are lies. If they had enough information to convict you, they would not be questioning you. You are always better off not talking.

Some common lies include:
   --'If you aren't guilty, why don't you talk?' They want to make you try to defend yourself, but whether or not you are 'guilty', you are better off not talking. Anything you say will be misquoted and used against you and if you answer some questions now

but stop talking later they will use that as evidence against you.

--'We already have your friends, it's only a matter of time before they reveal your involvement and then you're in bigger trouble' or 'If you don't cooperate, your friend is getting a longer prison sentence.' They very likely do not have your friends, do not have any proof or evidence that your friends were involved, do not have names of your friends, and do not have proof that you were involved.

--'Your friend revealed your involvement. You have no reason to be loyal to him. Tell us what he did and we'll give you a lighter sentence.' Your friend probably did not reveal anything about you. They are telling him/her the same thing that they are telling you. They want to turn you against each other. They likely have not even captured any of your friends and they likely do not have solid proof against anyone, even you.

--'Your friends set you up. They are laughing at you for getting caught.' This is another attempt to turn you and your friends against each other. If they have any of your friends, they are telling them the same thing.

--'If you don't talk now, we'll come back with a subpoena.' This

is usually an empty threat. They approached you without a subpoena because they do not have enough evidence to get one. If you talk, you might give them the information that they need to get one. If they do get a subpoena, which is unlikely if you stay silent, there are ways to legally/politically fight it. If you are in this situation, contact the National Lawyers Guild (http://www.nlg.org/).

--'We can't help you until you start helping us.' This is just another lie and tactic to get information.

--'We know you didn't do anything, we just want to clear it up.' or 'We know it was all your friend's idea.' Yet another lie. They probably did not even catch your friend.

--'Talk and we'll go easy on you. Talk and we'll give you bail. Talk and we'll give you a lighter sentence. Talk and we'll give you no sentence. Talk and we'll drop your charges.' These are all lies. They have lied, they do lie, and they will always lie. They are legally allowed to lie. They will do anything to get information out of you.

--'We already have all of the information we need to convict you.' If that were true, they would have already convicted you.

--'Give us information about your friends and we will give you a lighter sentence. We will give you no sentence. We will drop your charges entirely.' If they try to get information about other activists, SAY NOTHING. Do not give them information about other activists because doing so could get them arrested and probably will not do much for you even if the cops say that it will. If other activists go to prison because of you, not only will you feel guilty for sentencing a friend to prison, but the entire Liberation movement will never accept you back and you will be preventing your friends from saving countless animals. (More total prison time will be spent if you turn in your friends.) Turning in your friends also proves that you are responsible for the action. If you do not provide any information, you will likely have your own charges dropped.

--'You are intelligent, you have a good future, you seem like a good kid. You don't want to destroy your life like this, do you?' THEY DO NOT CARE ABOUT YOU. THEY JUST WANT YOU TO TALK. Say nothing. Again, your charges will probably be dropped because they do not have enough information to convict you.

--'The extremists hurt your movement. They turn people off to Animal Rights. Tell us who they are.' You should know that extremism helps. It is radicalism, direct action, and extremism that freed the Jews from Nazi concentration camps, freed the slaves, won equal rights for Africans and for women, and won every other social justice movement.

--'I support your goals, but not your/your friends' tactics.' Again, extremism and direct action work. Do not betray your friends and the movement. Betraying your friends also proves that you are involved so remaining silent is also in your own best interest.

-Some cops and agents will seem nice and pretend to be on your side. DO NOT TRUST THEM. After all, they will not get very far if they act like they are out to get you and like they hate animals. They try to trick you. Do not feel bad about telling them that you have nothing to say and to leave you alone. They are used to hearing it and will eventually get tired of your noncooperation and leave. No Compromise puts it nicely: 'In nearly every law enforcement encounter, you are viewed as if you are guilty, as if you have something to hide, as if you are a criminal. Read that again. Nothing you say can or will dissuade a law enforcement officer who is already suspicious of you. After all, why would s/he believe you? You are the suspect! And once you're being questioned, you're already a suspect. Read that again, too. It's a false hope to think that by talking to them you will convince them that you're a nice person. All you're accomplishing is convincing them that you're an idiot-a dupe-someone who, when pressured enough, will begin to talk. And now they will know to turn on the pressure.'

-They will play good cop/bad cop. One will use threats and the other will be nice and maybe promise to lighten your sentence. The bad cop might act so angry that he looks like he is about to use violence. The good cop will then tell the bad cop to leave the room and calm down. The good cop will say that the bad cop will come back to make good on his threats and that you should admit guilt now. THESE ARE ALL LIES AND EMPTY THREATS. IN REALITY, BOTH COPS ARE BAD COPS.

-They will ask you the same question multiple times, say 'Didn't you say that ... ?' and try to poke holes in your story. They will do this in attempt to get information and so that they can charge you with lying to a police officer.

-They will try to befriend you and make you feel rude by not answering questions. This applies to police and FBI and tends to occur at aboveground protests. Tell them that you have nothing to say and ignore them even if you are doing nothing illegal. Do not feel bad about it. They are used to hearing it and will go away.

-If you are taken to the police station or prison, they will interrogate you when you are tired because people are more likely to give out information when they are tired.

-If you are taken to the police station or prison, they will offer you drinks because people are more likely to give out information when they have to go to the bathroom.

-They will threaten to give you a longer sentence if you do not cooperate. Your sentence will probably be longer if you do cooperate while if you do not cooperate the charges will very likely be dropped because they do not have sufficient evidence to convict you. They will pretend that they have proof but in reality they have hardly anything.

-They will threaten to use physical violence. Threats of physical violence are almost always lies. If they do use physical violence, sue them. Do not fight back or you will be charged with assault on an officer and probably get hurt worse than if you do not fight back.

-They may threaten to give you a grand jury subpoena if you do not talk. They might give you one anyway and anything that you say now will allow for more detailed questions later. If you are given a subpoena, call a lawyer or the National Lawyers Guild (http://www.nlg.org/) immediately. Tell the National Lawyers Guild and other activists and friends about your subpoena. Do not try to deal with it alone.

-Remember: Stay calm and exercise your right to remain silent. Answer all questions with 'no comment' or 'I have nothing to say' other than name, address, and date of birth.

-The most important thing is to not say anything about anyone else. No matter how innocent it might seem, anything that you say about someone else, or about an action, could be used to arrest your friends. This means that they go to prison and cannot save any more animals for years and you are responsible for it.

-For more information on your legal rights, refer to the links under Further Reading.

Resisting the Urge to Talk
from NAALPO:
In order to resist the urge to talk, there are a few things you can do:

--Be mentally prepared: Envision what a visit would be like ahead of time. This he lps you remain calm and collected, and allows you to recite your actions – shutting your mouth and the door. Just expect to get a knock, get raided, even get hauled down to the local police precinct for questioning. It makes you more prepared if it does happen. Also be prepared to stare at the wall for hours if it does happen- remember, no one can make you open your mouth and expel air across your vocal cords to form words they want to hear. It is possible to look another human in the eye and simply stare without saying a word. It makes you uncomfortable, but its even worse for the oppressors.

--Plan on not caring if they come-ah-knockin': If you are an effective activist, there is a possibility, even a probability, they'll visit you. Just remember, their job is to oppress you and your community, and high on their agenda is to impede social change. By not talking, you strengthen your community and the movement.

--Don't let cops/agents scare you: Nothing is worse than buying into the authorities scare tactics. If they have you paranoid and scared, they have won. Just remember the silent treatment frustrates the authorities but saves activists. If they had evidence you had committed a crime, they would arrest you, not come around asking questions. And if cops scare you, just think what the animals must feel when they are hauled out of their cages to be tortured or killed. That's something to be afraid of, not some overweight bully of a law enforcement officer asking questions.

--Never let them see you sweat: Being overly concerned, even among friends or on the phone, will lead the authorities to your door. They will suspect you as a weak link and easy target. Keep your eye on the ball, animal suffering that we must stop using whatever means are at our disposal. Cops are just an ugly distraction.

--Never keep it a secret: If you are not sure what to do, ask an lawyer or activist friends. Don't keep visits, calls or letters a secret and always alert (without scaring!) other activists and friends in the community.

Arrest
This section is written from a United States perspective. International laws vary. For a walkthrough of UK arrests, refer to 'At The Cop Shop' near the bottom of this (http://www.animalliberationfront. com/ALFront/Activist%20Tips/Action%20Stations.htm) page.

-If cops attempt to arrest you, decide whether to resist or go along with it. If you are unmasked you should probably go along with it. If you are masked (whether taking underground direct action or are at an aboveground protest), you may choose to fight back and run, especially if you and your friends outnumber the police. If you choose to do this, you will be charged with resisting arrest and, if you physically contact a cop, assault on an officer. Make sure that the police do not manage to pull off your mask or bandanna. Get out of the area as quickly as possible. They will be looking for you. Do not use this tactic lightly.

-If you get arrested or if you and your friends resist arrest and you get caught, shout out your name (use your fake name or number which was chosen during the planning stage) so that your friends know who was caught. Make sure that your friends also know to do this.

-If you are arrested, try to remember the names and badge numbers of the arresting officers. You will probably be taken to the nearest police station. If you are arrested for underground direct action, if possible, get rid of tools, gloves, and masks, but not if it means leaving them where they can be found.

-You may want to consider using a fake name and address if you are interrogated and/or arrested. This is illegal so be extremely careful. If you do this, make sure that the person living at the address you use knows what name you will be using. This should be someone who supports direct action and will not turn you in. This person should agree to this before you take action. Talk about this in a secure location. A note by their phone will help them remember your fake name. Warn them that they might get a visit from the cops because visits to the houses of people who have been arrested are common. Ensure that they do not have militant literature, direct action guides, or anything else that cops should not see lying around. Make sure that this person knows to not let them in without a warrant. Again, this is illegal. Use this tactic with extreme caution.

-Stay calm. If you are arrested for aboveground activism, or even for underground direct action if you were not caught in the act, your charges will very likely be dismissed, and you will be much better off and less likely to give incriminating information if you stay calm. Your fear and anxiety are weaknesses that the police will exploit. Over time everything will clear up in your mind. Just remember, STAY SILENT. Say that you want to talk to a lawyer. Say nothing more (besides name, address, and date of birth) until you talk to your lawyer. DO NOT SAY ANYTHING ABOUT YOUR FRIENDS. DO NOT GIVE NAMES.

-Plead 'not guilty' to all charges, whether or not you are guilty. In some situations, pleading guilty or accepting a plea bargain might be in your best interest, but do not do this until after talking to trustworthy lawyers and, if possible, other activists.

-If you are arrested but your friends are not, deal with it. DO NOT TURN THEM IN. If your friends are not arrested, the cops probably do not have solid proof against you either, and you will soon be released if and only if you do not talk. If they do have enough evidence against you, although you might get a lighter sentence for turning in your friends, it is not worth it--not when it means your friends are imprisoned, they cannot help animals anymore, they will permanently be on the government's records, and you will be forever rejected by the Liberation movement. YOU WILL BE RE-SPONSIBLE FOR THEIR ARREST AND IMPRISONMENT. You also may not be given a lighter sentence for snitching even if you are told that you will. Do not do something that you will regret later.

-If you are caught, do not start blaming or arguing with your cellmates. This will prove that you are all responsible for the action. It will also cause infighting within the Liberation move-ment which is one of the movement's biggest weaknesses. You are all in this together and it is up to all of you to stay secure.

-When you get to the police station, politely beg to go to the bath-room. Wash your hands, stains, cuts, shoes, and anything else that can be used to connect you to the action. If you have anything that is incriminating and is small enough, flush it down the toilet.

-If arrested, you have the right to make free local calls to a law-yer, a bail bondsman, and a friend or relative. Demand this right.

-You have the right to a lawyer. If you cannot afford a law-yer, one will be appointed to you. Demand this right. For more information on your right to a lawyer, refer to this (http://www. criminalinfonetwork.com/right-attorney.htm) page.

-If you are responsible for what you are convicted of, do not tell your lawyer.

-They might question you when you are tired because people are more likely to give out information when they are tired.

-They might offer you drinks because people are more likely to give out information when they have to go to the bathroom.

-If they try to interview you, answer all questions with 'no comment'. If you accidentally say anything else, stop talking as soon as you catch yourself.

-If they try to make you fill out questionnaires or anything else, refuse.

-If you need a doctor while in custody, see one and get your injuries recorded. If you were assaulted by police, go to the hospital as soon as you are released if they do not let you go sooner. Make an appointment to see a lawyer and sue the police.

-If you are taken to jail or prison, tell the workers that you are Vegan as soon as you arrive so that they can provide you with Vegan food. They are legally required to provide adequate Vegan meals to Vegan prisoners but they do not always follow this law. If they do not, make it known through phone calls and letters to friends and relatives so that this information can be distributed among the Liberation movement. Activists will call in and write demanding that you are given adequate Vegan meals. After you refuse to eat non-Vegan food for long enough and they get enough phone calls and letters, they will cooperate, but you may not have much to eat for the first few days or even weeks. For the animals, stay strong and stay Vegan. Do not give in.

-If your lawyer says that you will get a lighter sentence by talking, get a new lawyer.

-If you admit to an action (which is NOT recommended), you have two options. If you act very sorry and say that you have learned your lesson and will not do it again, you will very likely get a lighter sentence. If you do not want to apologize to your enemies, tell them that you have no regrets about what you have done. Give a good speech.

-Remember that others have been through the same thing you are going through and survived. Think about the action (if you took direct action) and the animals you saved but do not speak of it. Think about other activists and their victories and anything else that you can draw strength from. Remember that a little jail time is nothing compared to the suffering that innocent animals are forced to endure on a daily basis.

-If arrested, remember: Stay calm, exercise your right to remain silent (answering all questions with 'no comment' or 'I have nothing to say', other than name, address, and date of birth), and lawyer. Plead 'not guilty' to all charges. Sign nothing and make no statements. It is better to make the police mad by being quiet than to give them information that can be used to imprison you and/or your friends.

-The most important thing is to not say anything about anyone else. No matter how innocent it might seem, anything that you say about someone else, or an action, could be used to arrest your friends. This means that they go to prison and cannot save any more animals for years and YOU ARE RESPONSIBLE FOR IT.

Grand Jury
This section is written from a United States perspective. International laws vary. UK activists should refer to Free BEAGLES (http://www.freebeagles.org/).

-DO NOT COOPERATE WITH GRAND JURY. Do not say anything to grand jury whether or not you are responsible for what you are convicted of. Do not tell the truth and do not lie. Do not even say things that you know cannot harm you. This is for your own good and for the good of other activists. Anything you say will be used against you regardless of how harmless it seems.

-You will probably go to jail for not cooperating with the grand jury but you will still very likely be much better off than if you cooperate. The longest sentence that you could get (if you are not convicted, which requires that you do not cooperate) is the length of the grand jury term. Grand juries usually have 18 month terms but they can be as low as 12 months or be extended to 24 months. Special grand juries can be extended to 36 months

94

but are only used to investigate 'organized crime'.

-Because of the leaderless, unstructured nature of the Liberation underground, it is unlikely that special grand juries will be used against Liberation activists. A grand jury term is short compared to the many years that you, or anyone convicted because of your cooperation, could face if you are convicted of a 'crime'.

-The grand jury is allowed to jail you in order to convince you to talk but not as punishment. Therefore, if you do not say nothing at all, not even harmless things, you will be far more likely to be released early.

-Talk only to your lawyer. If you are responsible for what you are convicted of, do not even tell your lawyer. If your lawyer suggests that you talk to grand jury, get a new lawyer. When talking to your lawyer, your conversation is supposed to be private. However, that does not mean that it is, so assume that the police, FBI, and judges are watching and listening (via wiretap, camera, or any other means).

-Your fifth amendment constitutional right to remain silent and right against self incrimination are taken away in grand jury. You are legally required to cooperate. Use those rights anyway and refuse to cooperate.

-If you answer 'harmless' questions and are then asked questions that could get you or your friends imprisoned, it will be suspicious if you stop talking after you have already answered some questions, and you will face heavy charges if you are caught lying to grand jury.

-By refusing to answer questions, regardless of whether or not you are responsible for what you are convicted of, in addition to saving yourself and your friends from potential heavy fines and long prison sentences, you will be taking a stand against government oppression, strengthening the movement, and making it easier for future activists to resist grand jury and avoid imprisonment. For more information on grand juries, refer to the links under Further Reading.

Preparing Yourself

Prior to becoming involved in direct action (including protests where you risk arrest), prepare yourself physically. Work out regularly. Do not use drugs or alcohol. They sedate your mind and body, cloud your judgement, slow your reflexes, and make you a target for police investigations.

-Be in very good health and top physical shape. You need to have a lot of strength, endurance, and agility. Train yourself to always have an alert mind and quick reflexes. If you are chased by a cop, can you outrun and outmaneuver him? Can you scale a barbed wire fence?

-Practice using equipment such as bolt cutters and lock picks. Practice parkour, such as climbing and jumping fences and walls,kong vaulting, jumping streams, and swimming across rivers.

-Practice anything else that you can think of. There are a lot of You-Tube videos that demonstrate how to do vaults, scale walls, and do similar things. Get to the point where you can scale large fences and walls gracefully and quickly--faster than cops will be able to. Even something as simple as walking or running outside at night while wearing a mask, headlamp, and backpack is important to practice. Do not let anyone see you training or practicing suspicious things. All training should be done in a house, in a garage, or in the country.

-It is also important to prepare yourself mentally. If you are interrogated by an agent, can you ignore threats and remain silent? Can you live with the knowledge that, at any time, you could be arrested and given a prison sentence? If you are arrested and bribed to turn in your friends, can you resist, even if it means a longer prison sentence for yourself? If a farmer wakes up when you are raiding his farm and approaches you with a gun, can you remain calm?

-Once you make the decision to become involved in the Liberation underground, there is no turning back. You will have a very hard and stressful life, living under a constant threat of interrogation and arrest. You will also be saving the lives of countless innocent beings. Choose wisely.

Further Reading

Some ALF pages do not load correctly in Firefox, Chrome, or Safari. If you are having problems, use Internet Explorer.

General Security, Protection, And Self Defense: (http://www.animalliberationfront.com/ALFront/Activist%20Tips/Security/Security_Protection_and_Self_Defense.htm)

Animal Liberation Primer (http://animalliberationpressoffice.org/publications%20online/ALprimer3.pdf)

ALF Primer (http://www.animalliberationfront.com/ALFront/ALFPrime.htm)

Going Underground (http://www.animalliberationfront.com/ALFront/Activist%20Tips/GoingUnderground.htm)

Getting Involved (http://www.animalliberationfront.com/ALFront/Activist%20Tips/LettersfromUnderground1.htm)

Finding A Partner (http://www.animalliberationfront.com/ALFront/Activist%20Tips/LettersfromUnderground2.htm)

Funding Your Actions (http://www.animalliberationfront.com/ALFront/Activist%20Tips/LettersfromUnderground3.htm)

Personal Liability (http://www.animalliberationfront.com/ALFront/Activist%20Tips/ShadowActivist1.htm)

Planning And Stealth (http://www.animalliberationfront.com/ALFront/Activist%20Tips/ShadowActivist2.htm)

Billboard Liberations (http://www.animalliberationfront.com/ALFront/Activist%20Tips/ShadowActivist3.htm)

Militant Tactics For Activists (http://negotiationisover.com/direct-action/tools-for-activists/)

Subversion For Dummies (http://negotiationisover.com/subversion-for-dummies/)

Targeting Companies Animal Rights Style (http://negotiationisover.com/2010/05/29/targeting-companies-animal-rights-style/)

Research For Radicals (http://security.resist.ca/personal/pdfs/researchguide.pdf)

Researching A Target (http://www.hackcanada.com/ice3/misc/ustarget.html)

Security
Security Culture (http://negotiationisover.com/direct-action/security-culture/)

Activists Find GPS Tracking Devices On Their Cars (http://lists.envirolink.org/pipermail/ar-news/Week-of-Mon-20030714/003630.html)

How To Detect GPS Spy Detectors (http://www.ehow.com/how_5698634_detect-gps-spy-detectors.html?ref=fuel&utm_source=yahoo&utm_medium=ssp&utm_campaign=yssp_art)

How To Detect GPS Tracking Devices (http://www.ehow.com/how_5118417_detect-gps-tracking-devices.html?ref=fuel&utm_source=yahoo&utm_medium=ssp&utm_campaign=yssp_art)

How To Detect GPS Tracking Units (http://www.gps-auto-trackers.com/trackingunits.html)

Frequency Finder Bug Detector Pro With GPS Tracking Detection (http://www.brickhousesecurity.com/gps-detector-frequency-finder.html)

ZC 270 Radio Frequency Detector (http://www.brickhousesecurity.com/abc-zc270zc270rfdetector.html)

Brick House Security Bug Detectors (http://www.brickhousesecurity.com/rf-transmitter-wireless-bug-camera-detectors.html)

Spy Hawk Pro Radio Frequency Detector (http://www.spyassociates.com/spy-hawk-pro-rf-phone-tap-detector-p-1962.html)

JM-20F Radio Frequency Detector (http://www.protectmefirst.com/detail.asp?PRODUCT_ID=RFD)

Spy Centre Security Bug Detectors (http://www.spycentre.com/bug_detectors.htm)

Computer Security
Computer Security (http://negotiationisover.com/2010/03/04/computer-security/)

TrueCrypt (http://www.truecrypt.org/downloads)

Ubuntu (http://www.ubuntu.com/)

MAC Changer (http://www.alobbs.com/macchanger)

Firefox (http://www.mozilla.com/)

Tor (https://www.torproject.org/)

Tor Browser (http://www.torproject.org/torbrowser/)

Riseup.net (https://riseup.net/)

PGP (http://www.pgp.com/)

PGP For Dummies (http://negotiationisover.com/2010/07/01/pgp-for-dummies-the-tutorial/)

GPG (http://www.gnupg.org/)

Enigform (https://addons.mozilla.org/en-US/firefox/addon/4531/)

FireGPG (https://addons.mozilla.org/en-US/firefox/addon/4645/)

Eraser (http://eraser.heidi.ie/download.php)

Bypassing Security
MIT Guide To Lock Picking (http://www.lockpickguide.com/MIT-guidetolockpicking.html)

Lock Picking (http://www.textfiles.com/anarchy/LOCKPICKING/)

Burglar Alarm Bypassing Part 1 (http://www.textfiles.com/anarchy/SCAMS/burglar1.txt)

Burglar Alarm Bypassing Part 2 (http://www.textfiles.com/anarchy/SCAMS/burglar2.txt)

Burglar Alarm Bypassing Part 3 (http://www.textfiles.com/anarchy/SCAMS/burglar3.txt)

Protests
Basic First Aid And Street Medics (http://www.animalliberationfront.com/ALFront/Activist%20Tips/Security/Street_Medics.htm)

Black Bloc, Security, Police Tactics, And Defense (http://negotiationisover.com/2010/01/10/security-culture-black-blocs-police-tactics-and-defense/)

5 Reasons For Activists To Cover Their Faces At Protests (http://www.greenisthenewred.com/blog/5-reasons-for-activists-to-cover-their-faces-at-protests/1082/)

Handy Tips (http://www.animalliberationfront.com/ALFront/Activist%20Tips/Handy%20Tips%20for%20Activists.html)

Actions For One (http://www.animalliberationfront.com/Practical/Shop--ToDo/Activism/Actionsfor1.htm)

Legal (specific to United States)
National Lawyers Guild (http://www.nlg.org/)

Civil Liberties Defense Center (http://www.cldc.org/)

American Civil Liberties Union (http://www.aclu.org/)

Guide To Operation Backfire (http://nlg.org/Operation%20Backfire.pdf)

Know Your Rights (http://www.cldc.org/knowyourrights.pdf)

Your Rights (http://www.animalliberationfront.com/ALFront/Activist%20Tips/Security/Know_Your_Rights_with_the_Man.htm)

Know Your Rights And Resist The Police State (http://www.animalliberationfront.com/ALFront/Activist%20Tips/KnowYourRights.htm)

If An Agent Knocks (http://security.resist.ca/personal/pdfs/IfanAgentKnocks.pdf)

Midnight Special Law Collective (http://midnightspecial.net/)

Criminal Information Network (http://www.criminalinfonetwork.com/)

Questions And Answers About Civil Disobedience And The Legal Process (http://www.nlg-la.org/index_files/cd_questions.pdf)

Green Is The New Red (http://www.greenisthenewred.com/blog/)

How The Patriot Act Re-Defines 'Domestic Terrorism' (http://www.aclu.org/natsec/emergpowers/14444leg20021206.html)

Animal Enterprise Terrorism 101 (http://www.greenisthenewred.com/blog/aeta-101/313/)

Animal Enterprise Terrorism Act (http://www.cldc.org/AETA.html)

Animal Enterprise Terrorism Act Tri-Fold (http://www.cldc.org/pdf/AETA%20trifold%20front%26back.pdf)

Grand Jury (specific to United States)
Grand Jury Zine (http://www.animalliberationfront.com/ALFront/Activist%20Tips/grandjuryzine.pdf)

Grand Jury Resistance (http://grandjuryresistance.org/)

Walkthrough Of A Grand Jury (http://www.animalliberationfront.com/ALFront/Activist%20Tips/Security/Walking_through_a_Grand_Jury.htm)

How To Crush A Grand Jury (http://nocompromise.org/issues/06crushgj.html)

ALF Suspect Refuses To Testify To Grand Jury (http://voiceofthevoiceless.org/possible-alf-investigation-activist-refuses-to-testify/)

Grand Jury Transcript Of Justin Samuel (http://www.scribd.com/full/5496528?access_key=key-29pallxov8tmwdvu0vjh)

If you are going to get involved in the Liberation underground, re-read this guide. Read it ten more times. Read every article on the ALF site and the pages linked to in the Further Reading section of this guide. Re-read the good articles. Re-re-read the good articles. Read the best articles ten more times. Make everyone in your cell do the same thing. It is better to spend a few hours reading and memorizing, or even a week of solid research, than to spend years in prison not helping animals!

* 9 7 8 0 9 8 3 0 5 4 7 0 2 *